Item	Qnty.	Description	
C1162		Concrete (N Scale) 2 ea.	
C1163		Masonry Arch (N Scale) 2 ea.	
C1164		Random Stone (N Scale) 2 ea.	
C1165		Timber (N Scale) 2 ea.	
TALUS			
C1270		Fine Buff	
C1271		Medium Buff	2.69
C1272		Coarse Buff	2.69
C1273		Extra Coarse Buff	2.69
C1274		Fine Brown	2.69
C1275		Medium Brown	2.69
C1276		Coarse Brown	2.69
C1277		Extra Coarse Brown	2.69
C1278		Fine Gray	2.69
C1279		Medium Gray	2.69
C1280		Coarse Gray	2.69
C1281		Extra Coarse Gray	2.69
C1282		Fine Natural	2.69
C1283		Medium Natural	2.69
C1284		Coarse Natural	2.69
C1285		Extra Coarse Natural	2.69
BULK LIGHTWEIGHT HYDROCAL			
C1201B		Bulk Lightweight Hydrocal** 5 gal	18.98
BOOKS/VIDEO			
C1207		Scenery Manual	9.98
R100		Woodland Scenics Buyer's Guide	1.50
R990		"The Clinic Video"	24.95
ST1401		SubTerrain Video	24.98
ST1402		SubTerrain How-To-Book	4.98
SCENE KITS			
SCENIC DETAILS			
D201		20 Tombstones	4.98
D202		Trackside Junk	4.98
D203		Crates - Barrels - Sacks	4.98
D204		15 Assorted Skids	4.98
D205		Assorted Junk Piles 15 pc.	4.98
D206		Assorted Mailboxes 17 pc.	4.98
D207		Disc & Tractor (1938 - 1946)	6.98
D208		Seeder & Tractor (1938 - 1946)	6.98
D209		"Aermotor" Windmill	6.98
D210		Plow, Disc, Horse and Man	6.98
D211		2 Tractors (1929 - 1938)	6.98
D212		3 Fuel Stands	6.98
D213		Smokehouse	8.49
D214		3 Outhouses and Man	8.49
D215		Chicken Coop	8.49
D216		Tool Shed	8.49
D217		Service Truck (1914 Diamond T)	8.49
D218		Grain Truck (1914 Diamond T)	8.49
D219		Ice House	11.98
D220		Daniels Outfitters	11.98
D221		Pharmacy	11.98
D222		Ticket Office	11.98
D223		Gas Station	11.98
D224		Doctor's Office and Shoe Repair	11.98
D225		Industrial Junk	4.98

MW01615446

Item	Description	Price
	...... Scale	6.98
D232	Diesel Fuel Facility	6.98
D233	Bulldozer	8.4
D234	Motor Grader	8.4
D235	Track Type Loader	8.4
D236	Gazebo	8.49
D237	Back Hoe - INSLEY Model K	11.98
D238	Rocky's Tavern	11.98
D239	Flag Depot	11.98
D240	Tucker Brothers - Machine Shop	11.98
D241	Branch Line Water Tower	11.98
D242	Tank Truck (Diamond T)	8.98
D243	Rural Sawmill	8.49
D244	Flat Bed & Tractor (Diamond T)	8.98
D246	Hyster Logging Cruiser & Tractor	11.98
D247	Dump Truck (1 1/2 Ton Federal)	8.98
D248	Street and Traffic Lights	6.98
COMPLETE SCENE KITS		
S130	Smiley's Tow Service	24.98
S131	Maple Leaf Cemetery	24.98
S132	Memorial Park	24.98
S1485	Town and Factory Building Set	98.00
TRACKSIDE SCENES		
TS151	Possum Hollow	24.98
TS152	Caboose and Sand Facility	24.98
TS153	Otis Coal Company	29.98
TS154	Tie & Plank Mill	29.98
MINI-SCENES		
M101	Abandoned Log Cabin	9.98
M102	Moonshine Still	9.98
M103	The Windmill	9.98
M104	The Hunter	9.98
M105	The Sign Painter	9.98
M106	The Tack Shed	9.98
M107	Tommy's Treehouse	9.98
M108	Outhouse Mischief	9.98
M109	Ernie's Fruit Stand	9.98
M110	Saturday Night Bath	9.98
M111	Floyd's Barber Shop	9.98
M112	Tractor Pit Stop	9.98
M125	Paint Set	4.49
M126	Pewter Patina Finish (dealer pk. 5 btl.)	1.98
M127	3" Dome & Base (dealer pk. 4)	6.98
DRY TRANSFER DECALS		
MODEL GRAPHICS		
MG701	Roman R.R. - B 1/16" to 5/16"	3.98
MG702	Roman R.R. - W 1/16" to 5/16"	3.98
MG703	Roman R.R. - G 1/16" to 5/16"	3.98
MG704	Roman R.R. - R 1/16" to 5/16"	3.98
MG705	Roman R.R. - Y 1/16" to 5/16"	3.98
MG706	Roman R.R. - S 1/16" to 5/16"	3.98
MG707	No. Roman R.R. -B 1/16" to 5/16"	3.98

Note: *B = Black   W = White   Y = Yellow   S = Silver   G = Gold   R =*

Item	Qnty.	Description	Price	Amt.
ST1409		4" Riser - 2' ea. 2/pkg.	7.98	
ST1410		2% Incline Sets (0 - 4" rise 16')	12.98	
ST1416		3% Incline Sets (0 - 4" rise 12')	10.98	
ST1411		4% Incline Sets (0 - 4" rise 8')	7.98	
ST1412		2% Incline Starter - 2' ea. 8/pkg.	3.98	
...15		3% Incline Starter - 2' ea. 6/pkg.	3.98	
		4% Incline Starter - 2' ea. 4/pkg.	3.98	
		8" Profile Boards - 2' ea.	6.98	
		1/4" Foam Sheet - 2'	2.98	
		1/2" Foam Sheet - 2'	2.98	
		1" Foam Sheet - 2'	3.49	
...5		2" Foam Sheet - 1 pc. 2'	6.98	
...26		3" Foam Sheet - 1 pc. 2'	9.98	
...427		4" Foam Sheet - 1 pc. 2'	12.98	
TOOLS				
...T1431		Foam Pencils 4/pkg.	3.98	
ST1432		Foam Nails - 2" nails 75/pkg.	4.98	
ST1433		Foam Knife	5.98	
ST1434		Foam Knife Blades 4/pkg.	4.98	
ST1435		Hot Wire Foam Cutter	29.98	
ST1436		Hot Wire Replacement Wire 4'	1.98	
ST1437		Foam Cutter Bow & Guide	7.49	
GLUES				
ST1444		Foam Tack Glue 12 oz.	9.98	
ST1445		Low Temp Foam Glue Gun	16.98	
ST1446		Low Temp Foam Glue 10/pkg.	3.98	
ROAD SYSTEM				
ST1452		Smooth-It 1 qt.	3.98	
ST1453		Top Coat Asphalt 4 oz.	3.98	
ST1454		Top Coat Concrete 4 oz.	3.98	
ST1455		Paving Tape - 1/4" x 30'	5.98	
FILLING, COVERING & SEALING				
ST1447		Foam Putty 16 Oz.	7.98	
C1203		Plaster Cloth 10 sq. ft.	6.98	
C1205		Flex Paste 16 oz.	11.98	
TRACK-BED				
ST1460		N-Sheet Goods 6/pkg. (3 1/4" x 24")	7.44	
ST1470		HO & O-Sheet Goods 6/pkg. (5" x 24")	13.08	
ST1471		HO-2' ea. 12/pkg. (11 @ .78 + 1 free)	8.58	
ST1472		N-2' ea. 12/pkg. (11 @ .52 + 1 free)	5.72	
ST1473		O-2' ea. 12/pkg. (11 @ 1.15 + 1 free)	12.65	
BULK TRACK-BED				
ST1461		HO-2' ea. 36/pkg.(33 @ .78 + 3 free)	25.74	
ST1462		N-2' ea. 36/pkg. (33 @ .52 + 3 free)	17.16	
ST1463		O-2' ea. 36/pkg. (33 @ 1.15 + 3 free)	37.95	
SUBTERRAIN KIT				
ST1482		Scenic Ridge Layout Kit	198.00	
S1485		Town and Factory Building Set	98.00	
TERRAIN SYSTEM MATERIALS				
PLASTER PRODUCTS				
C1201		Lightweight Hydrocal* 1/2 gal.	7.49	
C1202		Mold-A-Scene Plaster 1/2 gal.	7.49	
C1203		Plaster Cloth approx. 10 sq. ft.	6.98	
TERRAIN ACCESSORIES				
C1204		Latex Rubber 16 oz.	9.98	
C1205		Flex Paste 16 oz.	11.98	
C1206		E-Z Water 16 oz.	8.49	
C1207		The Scenery Manual	9.98	

Item	Qnty.	Description	Price	Amt.
EARTH COLORS (LIQUID PIGMENT)				
C1215		Earth Color Kit 8 colors	14.98	
C1216		White 4 oz.	3.98	
C1217		Concrete 4 oz.	3.98	
C1218		Stone Gray 4 oz.	3.98	
C1219		Slate Gray 4 oz.	3.98	
C1220		Black 4 oz.	3.98	
C1221		Raw Umber 4 oz.	3.98	
C1222		Burnt Umber 4 oz.	3.98	
C1223		Yellow Ocher 4 oz.	3.98	
C1228		Green Undercoat 8 oz.	5.49	
C1229		Earth Undercoat 8 oz.	5.49	
ROCK MOLDS				
C1230		Outcroppings 5" x 7" mold	5.98	
C1231		Surface Rocks 5" x 7" mold	5.98	
C1232		Boulders 5" x 7" mold	5.98	
C1233		Embankments 5" x 7" mold	5.98	
C1234		Random Rock 5" x 7" mold	5.98	
C1235		Laced Face Rock 5" x 7" mold	5.98	
C1236		Classic Rock 5" x 7" mold	5.98	
C1237		Wind Rock 5" x 7" mold	5.98	
C1238		Weathered Rock 5" x 7" mold	5.98	
C1239		Strata Stone 5" x 7" mold	5.98	
C1240		Rock Mass 5" x 7" mold	5.98	
C1241		Layered Rock 5" x 7" mold	5.98	
C1242		Washed Rock 10 1/2" x 5" mold	6.98	
C1243		Base Rock 10 1/2" x 5" mold	6.98	
C1244		Facet Rock 10 1/2" x 5" mold	6.98	
TUNNEL LINER FORM				
C1250		Tunnel Liner Form mold	3.49	
TUNNEL PORTALS				
C1252		Concrete (HO Scale) single	6.98	
C1253		Cut Stone (HO Scale) single	6.98	
C1254		Timber (HO Scale) single	6.98	
C1255		Random Stone (HO Scale) single	6.98	
C1256		Concrete (HO Scale) double	7.49	
C1257		Cut Stone (HO Scale) double	7.49	
C1152		Concrete (N Scale) 2 single	7.49	
C1153		Cut Stone (N Scale) 2 single	7.49	
C1154		Timber (N Scale) 2 single	7.49	
C1155		Random Stone (N Scale) 2 single	7.49	
C1156		Concrete (N Scale) 2 double	8.49	
C1157		Cut Stone (N Scale) 2 double	8.49	
RETAINING/WING WALLS				
C1258		Concrete (HO Scale) 3 ea.	6.98	
C1259		Cut Stone (HO Scale) 3 ea.	6.98	
C1260		Timber (HO Scale) 3 ea.	6.98	
C1261		Random Stone (HO Scale) 3 ea.	6.98	
C1158		Concrete (N Scale) 6 ea.	8.49	
C1159		Cut Stone (N Scale) 6 ea.	8.49	
C1160		Timber (N Scale) 6 ea.	8.49	
C1161		Random Stone (N Scale) 6 ea.	8.49	
CULVERTS				
C1262		Concrete (HO Scale) 2 ea.	6.49	
C1263		Masonry Arch (HO Scale) 2 ea.	6.49	
C1264		Random Stone (HO Scale) 2 ea.	6.49	
C1265		Timber (HO Scale) 2 ea.	6.49	

Item	Qnty.	Description	Price	Amt.
T1364		Medium Green	7.98	
T1365		Dark Green	7.98	
T1366		Conifer	7.98	
FALL COARSE TURF				
T1353		Yellow	7.98	
T1354		Orange	7.98	
T1355		Red	7.98	
T1356		Rust	7.98	
BALLAST 32 OZ. SHAKER BOTTLES				
B1372		Brown	Fine	7.98	
B1373		Buff	Fine	7.98	
B1374		Light Gray	Fine	7.98	
B1375		Gray	Fine	7.98	
B1376		Cinders	Fine	7.98	
B1379		Brown	Medium	7.98	
B1380		Buff	Medium	7.98	
B1381		Light Gray	Medium	7.98	
B1382		Gray	Medium	7.98	
B1383		Cinders	Medium	7.98	
B1386		Brown	Coarse	7.98	
B1387		Buff	Coarse	7.98	
B1388		Light Gray	Coarse	7.98	
B1389		Gray	Coarse	7.98	
B1390		Cinders	Coarse	7.98	
B1393		Gray Blend	Fine	7.98	
B1394		Gray Blend	Medium	7.98	
B1395		Gray Blend	Coarse	7.98	
STATIC GRASS FLOCK 32 OZ. SHAKER BOTTLES				
FL631		Wild Honey	7.98	
FL632		Harvest Gold	7.98	
FL633		Burnt Grass	7.98	
FL634		Light Green	7.98	
FL635		Medium Green	7.98	
FL636		Dark Green	7.98	
LICHEN				
L161		Spring Green	4.98	
L162		Light Green	4.98	
L163		Medium Green	4.98	
L164		Dark Green	4.98	
L165		Autumn Mix	4.98	
L166		Natural	4.98	
L167		Light Green Mix	9.98	
L168		Dark Green Mix	9.98	
CLUMP-FOLIAGE				
FC181		Burnt Grass	10.98	
FC182		Light Green	10.98	
FC183		Medium Green	10.98	
FC184		Dark Green	10.98	
FC185		Conifer Green	10.98	
FC186		Fall Mix	10.98	
REALISTIC TREES (READY MADE)				
GREEN DECIDUOUS				
TR1001		3/4" - 1 1/4" Med. Green	8/pkg.	5.98	
TR1002		1 1/4" - 2" Med. Green	5/pkg.	5.98	
TR1003		2" - 3" Light Green	4/pkg.	6.49	
TR1004		2" - 3" Medium Green	4/pkg.	6.49	
TR1005		2" - 3" Dark Green	4/pkg.	6.49	

Item	Qnty.	Description	Price	Amt.
TR1006		3" - 4" Light Green	3/pkg.	6.98	
TR1007		3" - 4" Medium Green	3/pkg.	6.98	
TR1008		3" - 4" Dark Green	3/pkg.	6.98	
TR1009		4" - 5" Light Green	3/pkg.	7.49	
TR1010		4" - 5" Medium Green	3/pkg.	7.49	
TR1011		4" - 5" Dark Green	3/pkg.	7.4	
TR1012		5" - 6" Light Green	2/pkg.	6.3	
TR1013		5" - 6" Medium Green	2/pkg.	6.9	
TR1014		5" - 6" Dark Green	2/pkg.	6.9	
TR1015		6" - 7" Light Green	2/pkg.	8.4	
TR1016		6" - 7" Medium Green	2/pkg.	8.4	
TR1017		6" - 7" Dark Green	2/pkg.	8.49	
TR1018		7" - 8" Medium Green	2/pkg.	10.49	
TR1019		8" - 9" Medium Green	2/pkg.	12.49	
FALL DECIDUOUS				
TR1040		1 1/4" - 3" Fall Mix	9/pkg.	11.49	
TR1041		3" - 5" Fall Mix	6/pkg.	13.49	
CONIFERS				
TR1060		2 1/2" - 4" Conifer Green	5/pkg.	6.98	
TR1061		4" - 6" Conifer Green	4/pkg.	6.98	
TR1062		6" - 7" Conifer Green	3/pkg.	7.49	
TR1063		7" - 8" Conifer Green	3/pkg.	9.49	
REALISTIC TREES (VALUE PACKS)				
MIXED GREEN DECIDUOUS				
TR1070		3/4" - 2" Green Decid.	38/pkg.	22.98	
TR1071		2" - 3" Green Decid.	23/pkg.	22.98	
TR1072		3" - 5" Green Decid.	14/pkg.	22.98	
MIXED FALL DECIDUOUS				
TR1075		3/4" - 2" Fall Decid.	38/pkg.	22.98	
TR1076		2" - 3" Fall Decid.	23/pkg.	22.98	
TR1077		3" - 5" Fall Decid.	14/pkg.	22.98	
CONIFERS				
TR1080		2 1/2"- 4" Con. Green	33/pkg.	22.98	
TR1081		4" - 6" Con. Green	24/pkg.	22.98	
TR1082		6" - 8" Con. Green	12/pkg.	22.98	
REALISTIC TREES (KITS)				
GREEN DECIDUOUS				
TR1101		Trees 3/4" - 3"	36/pkg.	13.98	
TR1102		Trees 3" - 5"	14/pkg.	13.98	
TR1103		Trees 5" - 7"	7/pkg.	13.98	
CONIFERS (CONIFER GREEN)				
TR1104		Pines 2 1/2" - 4"	42/pkg.	13.98	
TR1105		Pines 4" - 6"	24/pkg.	13.98	
TR1106		Pines 6" - 8"	16/pkg.	13.98	
SCENERY LEARNING KITS				
LK951		Rock Making	10.98	
LK952		Road Building	10.98	
LK953		Tree Making	10.98	
LK954		Landscaping	10.98	
SUBTERRAIN SYSTEM MATERIALS				
INSTRUCTIONAL MATERIALS				
ST1401		SubTerrain Video	24.98	
ST1402		SubTerrain How-To-Book	4.98	
FOAM PRODUCTS				
ST1406		1/2" Riser - 2' ea.	4/pkg.	3.98	
ST1414		3/4" Riser - 2' ea.	4/pkg.	4.98	
ST1407		1" Riser - 2' ea.	4/pkg.	5.98	
ST1408		2" Riser - 2' ea.	4/pkg.	7.98	

Item	Qnty.	Description		Price	Amt.
MG708		No. Roman R.R.-W	1/16" to 5/16"	3.98	
MG709		No. Roman R.R.-G	1/16" to 5/16"	3.98	
MG710		No. Roman R.R.-R	1/16" to 5/16"	3.98	
MG711		No. Roman R.R.-Y	1/16" to 5/16"	3.98	
MG712		No. Roman R.R.-S	1/16" to 5/16"	3.98	
MG713		Roman R.R. - B	3/8", 1/2"	3.98	
MG714		Roman R.R. - W	3/8", 1/2"	3.98	
MG715		Extended Roman-B	1/16", 1/4"	3.98	
MG716		Extended Roman-W	1/16", 1/4"	3.98	
MG717		Extended Roman-G	1/16", 1/4"	3.98	
MG718		Cond. Roman R.R.-B	1/16", 5/16"	3.98	
MG719		Cond. Roman R.R.-W	1/16", 5/16"	3.98	
MG720		Gothic R.R. - B	1/16", 5/16"	3.98	
MG721		Gothic R.R. - W	1/16", 5/16"	3.98	
MG722		Gothic R.R. - G	1/16", 5/16"	3.98	
MG723		Gothic R.R. - R	1/16", 5/16"	3.98	
MG724		Gothic R.R. - Y	1/16", 5/16"	3.98	
MG725		Gothic R.R. - S	1/16", 5/16"	3.98	
MG726		No. Gothic R.R. - B	1/16", 5/16"	3.98	
MG727		No. Gothic R.R. - W	1/16", 5/16"	3.98	
MG728		No. Gothic R.R. - G	1/16", 5/16"	3.98	
MG729		No. Gothic R.R. - R	1/16", 5/16"	3.98	
MG730		No. Gothic R.R. - Y	1/16", 5/16"	3.98	
MG731		No. Gothic R.R. - S	1/16", 5/16"	3.98	
MG732		Gothic R.R. - B	3/8", 1/2"	3.98	
MG733		Gothic R.R. - W	3/8", 1/2"	3.98	
MG734		Extended Gothic R.R.-B	1/16", 1/4"	3.98	
MG735		Extended Gothic R.R.-W	1/16", 1/4"	3.98	
MG736		Extended Gothic R.R.-G	1/16", 1/4"	3.98	
MG737		Cond. Gothic R.R.-B	1/16", 5/16"	3.98	
MG738		Cond. Gothic R.R.-W	1/16", 5/16"	3.98	
MG739		45° USA Gothic - B	1/16", 5/16"	3.98	
MG740		45° USA Gothic - W	1/16", 5/16"	3.98	
MG741		45° USA Gothic - R	1/16", 5/16"	3.98	
MG742		45° USA Gothic - Y	1/16", 5/16"	3.98	
MG743		45° USA Gothic - S	1/16", 5/16"	3.98	
MG744		45° USA Gothic - B	3/8", 1/2"	3.98	
MG745		45° USA Gothic - W	3/8", 1/2"	3.98	
MG746		No. 45° USA Gothic-B	1/16", 5/16"	3.98	
MG747		No. 45° USA Gothic-W	1/16", 5/16"	3.98	
MG748		No. 45° USA Gothic-R	1/16", 5/16"	3.98	
MG749		No. 45° USA Gothic-Y	1/16", 5/16"	3.98	
MG750		No. 45° USA Gothic-S	1/16", 5/16"	3.98	
MG751		Stencil/Block Rom.-B	3/32",1/8",1/4"	3.98	
MG752		Stencil/Block Rom.-W	3/32",1/8",1/4"	3.98	
MG753		Stencil/Block Rom.-R	3/32",1/8",1/4"	3.98	
MG754		Stencil/Block Rom.-Y	3/32",1/8",1/4"	3.98	
MG755		Script & Old English-B	3/16", 5/16"	3.98	
MG756		Script & Old English-W	3/16", 5/16"	3.98	
MG757		Script & Old English-G	3/16", 5/16"	3.98	
MG758		Script & Old English-S	3/16", 5/16"	3.98	
MG759		Stripes - B	.010" to 3/64"	3.98	
MG760		Stripes - W	.010" to 3/64"	3.98	
MG761		Stripes - G	.010" to 3/64"	3.98	
MG762		Stripes - R	.010" to 3/64"	3.98	

Item	Qnty.	Description		Price	Amt.
MG763		Stripes - Y	.010" to 3/64"	3.98	
MG764		Stripes - S	.010" to 3/64"	3.98	
RAILROAD/ADVERTISING DECALS					
D245		Series One/Dry Transfer Decals		4.98	
DT501		Tuscan & Playbill	3/16", 1/8"	3.49	
DT502		Beton Windson	3/32",1/8",3/16", 1/4"	3.49	
DT503		Goth. Outline/Sign Paint.	5/16",3/16"	3.49	
DT504		R.R. Rom.-R/G	1/16",3/32",1/8",3/16"	3.49	
DT505		R.R. Rom.-B	1/16",3/32",1/8",3/16"	3.49	
DT506		R.R. Roman-W	1/16",3/32",1/8",3/16"	3.49	
DT507		R.R. Gothic-W	1/16",3/32",1/8",3/16"	3.49	
DT508		R.R. Gothic-B	1/16",3/32",1/8",3/16"	3.49	
DT509		R.R. Rom. No.-B	1/16",3/32",1/8",3/16"	3.49	
DT510		R.R. Rom. No.-W	1/16",3/32",1/8",3/16"	3.49	
DT511		R.R. Goth. No.-B	1/16",3/32",1/8",3/16"	3.49	
DT512		R.R. Goth. No.-B	1/16",3/32",1/8",3/16"	3.49	
DT513		Stripes - B	1/64", 1/32", 1/16"	3.49	
DT514		Stripes - W	1/64", 1/32", 1/16"	3.49	
DT515		Stripes - R	1/64", 1/32", 1/16"	3.49	
DT516		Stripes - Y	1/64", 1/32", 1/16"	3.49	
DT551		Tavern, Gas Station & Com. Signs		4.98	
DT552		Assorted Business Signs		4.98	
DT553		Depot, R.E.A. & Advertising Signs		4.98	
DT554		Product & Advertising Signs		4.98	
DT555		Road, Product & Burmashave Signs		4.98	
DT556		Assorted Logos & Advertising Signs		4.98	
DT557		Data/Warn. Labels & Com. Signs		4.98	
DT558		Railroad Heralds		4.98	
DT559		Standard Oil & Business Signs		4.98	
DT560		Crate Labels & Warning Signs		4.98	
DT561		1960's Signs & Posters		4.98	
DT562		1950's Signs & Posters		4.98	
DT563		1940's Signs & Posters		4.98	
DT601		Box Car Data-Roman Black/White		3.49	
DT602		Box Car Data-Gothic Black/White		3.49	
DT603		Union Pacific Box Cars		3.49	
DT604		Santa Fe Box Cars-Passenger		3.49	
DT605		Santa Fe Box Cars		3.49	
DT606		Rock Island Box Car Soft Touch/DPE		3.49	
DT607		BN and CB & Q Box Cars		3.49	
DT608		Frisco Box Cars		3.49	
DT609		Southern Pacific Box Cars		3.49	
DT610		Great Northern Box Cars		3.49	
DT611		Reefer Cars Amour/Miller/Hormel		3.49	
DT600		Dry Transfer Burnisher		3.49	
MINI SERIES					
DT570		Product Logos		4.98	
DT571		Railroad Signs		4.98	
DT572		Business Signs		4.98	
DT573		Signs & Posters		4.98	
DT574		Service Station Sings		4.98	
DT575		Lettering, Black & White		3.49	
HOB-E-LUBE					
HL650		7-Pak Workbench Assortment		19.98	
HL651		Dry Graphite with Molybdenum		3.79	
HL652		Dry White Lube with Teflon***		3.79	

Red

Item	Qnty.	Description	Price	Amt.
		LANDSCAPE SYSTEM MATERIALS		
		TREE KITS		
TK11		2 1/4" Forked Trunk 4/kit	5.49	
TK12		2 1/2" Ornamental 5/kit	5.49	
TK13		2 1/2" Straight Trunk 5/kit	5.49	
TK14		3 1/4" Softwood Pine 5/kit	5.49	
TK17		3 1/2" Shag Bark 3/kit	5.49	
TK18		3 1/2" Double Fork 2/kit	5.49	
TK19		4" Shade Tree 2/kit	5.49	
TK20		4 1/2"Columnar Pine 4/kit	5.49	
TK21		4 1/2" Gnarled 2/kit	5.49	
TK22		Dead Trees 5/kit	5.49	
		LARGE TREE KITS		
TK23		6"-9" Pine Trees 5/kit	9.98	
TK24		Hedge Row Scene 24"-30" long	9.98	
TK25		5 1/2"-6 1/2" Hardwood 3/kit	9.98	
TK26		7"-7 1/2" Big Old Trees 2/kit	9.98	
		FOREST KITS		
TK27		2"-4" Pine Forest 24/kit	10.98	
TK28		2"-4" Hardwood Forest 24/kit	10.98	
		STUMPS, FRUIT, FLOWERS		
S31		Cut Stumps 14/pkg.	2.49	
S32		Broken Stumps 14/pkg.	2.49	
T47		Fruit - Apples and Oranges	2.59	
T48		Flowers - 4 colors	2.59	
		EXTRA COARSE TURF		
T34		Yellow Grass	2.79	
T35		Burnt Grass	2.79	
T36		Light Green	2.79	
T37		Medium Green	2.79	
T38		Dark Green	2.79	
T39		Conifer Green	2.79	
		FINE TURF		
T41		Soil	2.79	
T42		Earth	2.79	
T43		Yellow Grass	2.79	
T44		Burnt Grass	2.79	
T45		Green Grass	2.79	
T46		Weeds	2.79	
		BLENDED TURF		
T49		Green Blend	5.59	
T50		Earth Blend	5.59	
		COARSE TURF		
T60		Earth	2.79	
T61		Yellow Grass	2.79	
T62		Burnt Grass	2.79	
T63		Light Green	2.79	
T64		Medium Green	2.79	
T65		Dark Green	2.79	
		FOLIAGE		
F51		Light Green	2.98	
F52		Medium Green	2.98	
F53		Dark Green	2.98	
F54		Conifer Green	2.98	
F55		Early Fall Mix	2.98	
F56		Late Fall Mix	2.98	

Item	Qnty.	Description	Price	Amt
		FOLIAGE CLUSTERS		
FC57		Light Green	5.98	
FC58		Medium Green	5.98	
FC59		Dark Green	5.98	
		FIELD GRASS		
FG171		Natural Straw	2.79	
FG172		Harvest Gold	2.79	
FG173		Light Green	2.79	
FG174		Medium Green	2.79	
		LANDSCAPE ACCESSORIES		
SN140		Soft Flake Snow	7.98	
FP178		Poly Fiber - Green	2.29	
S191		Scenic Cement	5.49	
S192		Scenic Sprayer	3.29	
S193		Scenic Sifter	2.98	
S195		Hob-e-Tac Adhesive	4.79	
		BALLAST		
B70		Iron Ore Fine	2.69	
B71		Dark Brown Fine	2.69	
B72		Brown Fine	2.69	
B73		Buff Fine	2.69	
B74		Light Gray Fine	2.69	
B75		Gray Fine	2.69	
B76		Cinders Fine	2.69	
B77		Iron Ore Medium	2.69	
B78		Dark Brown Medium	2.69	
B79		Brown Medium	2.69	
B80		Buff Medium	2.69	
B81		Light Gray Medium	2.69	
B82		Gray Medium	2.69	
B83		Cinders Medium	2.69	
B84		Iron Ore Coarse	2.69	
B85		Dark Brown Coarse	2.69	
B86		Brown Coarse	2.69	
B87		Buff Coarse	2.69	
B88		Light Gray Coarse	2.69	
B89		Gray Coarse	2.69	
B90		Cinders Coarse	2.69	
B91		Dry Ballast Cement	2.99	
B92		Mine Run Coal	2.49	
B93		Lump Coal	2.49	
B94		Gray Blend Ballast 30 oz. med.	5.49	
		TURF 32 oz. SHAKER BOTTLES		
		FINE TURF		
T1341		Soil	7.98	
T1342		Earth	7.98	
T1343		Yellow Grass	7.98	
T1344		Burnt Grass	7.98	
T1345		Green Grass	7.98	
T1346		Weeds	7.98	
		BLENDED TURF		
T1349		Green Blend	7.98	
T1350		Earth Blend	7.98	
		COARSE TURF		
T1361		Yellow Grass	7.98	
T1362		Burnt Grass	7.98	
T1363		Light Green	7.98	

Item	Qnty.	Description		Price	Amt.
HL653		Ultra-Lite Oil		3.79	
HL654		Lite Oil		3.79	
HL655				3.79	
HL656				3.79	
HL657				3.79	
HL661		Ultra Lite Premium Oil		6.98	
HL662		Lite Premium Oil		6.98	
HL663		Medium Premium Oil		6.98	
HL664		Gear Lube Premium Oil		6.98	
HOB-BITS					
MACHINE SCREWS					
1801		00-90 1/8" Round Head	5/pkg.	1.49	
1802		00-90 1/4" Round Head	5/pkg.	1.49	
1803		00-90 3/8" Round Head	5/pkg.	1.49	
1804		00-90 1/2" Round Head	5/pkg.	1.49	
1805		0-80 1/8" Round Head	5/pkg.	1.49	
1806		0-80 1/4" Round Head	5/pkg.	1.49	
1807		0-80 3/8" Round Head	5/pkg.	1.49	
1808		0-80 1/2" Round Head	5/pkg.	1.49	
1809		1-72 1/8" Round Head	5/pkg.	1.49	
1810				1.49	
1811				1.49	
1812				1.49	
1813		2-56 1/8" Round Head	5/pkg.	1.49	
1814		2-56 1/4" Round Head	5/pkg.	1.49	
1815		2-56 3/8" Round Head	5/pkg.	1.49	
1816		2-56 1/2" Round Head	5/pkg.	1.49	
1821				1.49	
1822				1.49	
1823				1.49	
1824				1.49	
1825				1.49	
1826		0-80 1/4" Fillister Head	5/pkg.	1.49	
1827		0-80 3/8" Fillister Head	5/pkg.	1.49	
1828		0-80 1/2" Fillister Head	5/pkg.	1.49	
1829		1-72 1/8" Fillister Head	5/pkg.	1.49	
1830		1-72 1/4" Fillister Head	5/pkg.	1.49	
1831		1-72 3/8" Fillister Head	5/pkg.	1.49	
1832		1-72 1/2" Fillister Head	5/pkg.	1.49	
1833		2-56 1/8" Fillister Head	5/pkg.	1.49	
1834		2-56 1/4" Fillister Head	5/pkg.	1.49	
1835				1.49	
1836				1.49	
1841				1.49	
1842				1.49	
1843				1.49	
1844				1.49	
1845				1.49	
1846				1.49	
1847				1.49	
1848				1.49	
1849				1.49	
1850				1.49	
1851				1.49	
1852				1.49	

Item	Qnty.	Description		Price	Amt.
H853		2-56 1/8" Flat Head	5/pkg.	1.49	
H854		2-56 1/4" Flat Head	5/pkg.	1.49	
H855		2-56 3/8" Flat Head	5/pkg.	1.49	
H856		2-56 1/2" Flat Head	5/pkg.	1.49	
H861		00-90 1/8" Hex Head	5/pkg.	1.49	
H862		00-90 1/4" Hex Head	5/pkg.	1.49	
H863		00-90 3/8" Hex Head	5/pkg.	1.49	
H864		00-90 1/2" Hex Head	5/pkg.	1.49	
H865		0-80 1/8" Hex Head	5/pkg.	1.49	
H866		0-80 1/4" Hex Head	5/pkg.	1.49	
H867		0-80 3/8" Hex Head	5/pkg.	1.49	
H868		0-80 1/2" Hex Head	5/pkg.	1.49	
H869		1-72 1/8" Hex Head	5/pkg.	1.49	
H870		1-72 1/4" Hex Head	5/pkg.	1.49	
H871		1-72 3/8" Hex Head	5/pkg.	1.49	
H872		1-72 1/2" Hex Head	5/pkg.	1.49	
H873		2-56 1/8" Hex Head	5/pkg.	1.49	
H874		2-56 1/4" Hex Head	5/pkg.	1.49	
H875		2-56 3/8" Hex Head	5/pkg.	1.49	
H876		2-56 1/2" Hex Head	5/pkg.	1.49	
DIES					
H877		00-90 Die	1/pkg.	29.98	
H878		0-80 Die	1/pkg.	29.98	
H879		1-72 Die	1/pkg.	29.98	
H880		2-56 Die	1/pkg.	29.98	
HEX NUTS					
H881		00-90 Hex Nut	5/pkg.	1.49	
H882		0-80 Hex Nut	5/pkg.	1.49	
H883		1-72 Hex Nut	5/pkg.	1.49	
H884		2-56 Hex Nut	5/pkg.	1.49	
WRENCHES					
H885		00-90 Wrench	1/pkg.	4.49	
H886		0-80 Wrench	1/pkg.	4.49	
H887		1-72 Wrench	1/pkg.	4.49	
H888		2-56 Wrench	1/pkg.	4.49	
WASHERS					
H891		00-90 Washers	5/pkg.	1.49	
H892		0-80 Washers	5/pkg.	1.49	
H893		1-72 Washers	5/pkg.	1.49	
H894		2-56 Washers	5/pkg.	1.49	
TAPS					
H895		00-90 Tap	1/pkg.	3.29	
H896		0-80 Tap	1/pkg.	3.29	
H897		1-72 Tap	1/pkg.	3.29	
H898		2-56 Tap	1/pkg.	3.29	
COMPLETE LANDSCAPE KITS					
S926		Complete Landscape Kit		19.98	
S297		The Scenery Kit		39.98	
S928		Mountain Valley Scenery Kit		69.98	
S929		SubTerrain Scenery Kit		49.98	

* Hydrocal is a product of U.S. Gypsum
** Special Handling - add $12.00 per each 5 gal. bulk Hydrocal
*** Teflon is a Dupont registered trademark

Available at better hobby stores...world wide.

Prices subject to change without notice.

12/99

SubTerrain Manual

Library of Congress Catalog Card Number:
98-60966

ISBN..........1-887436-02-2

CONTENTS

Introduction

Create a realistic layout for your model railroad with the revolutionary SubTerrain System. This System includes high-density foam and all of the tools and accessories you will need. SubTerrain is extremely adaptable and expandable to your plans.

Building a layout with The SubTerrain System is extremely simple. It is also completely different from older methods of building model railroads. We recommend that you familiarize yourself with the entire process before beginning to use the SubTerrain System. Read through the entire book; then go back and follow the instructions step-by-step while you build your own model railroad.

 **TECH TIP**

Woodland Scenics has created a full-length video as a helpful companion to this book. Ask your retailer for a copy of *SubTerrain: A How-To-Video*.

Before You Begin

Before creating a model railroad, there are a few preparations to make. First you need a plan. A wide variety of track plans are available. Many magazines, books and other publications feature track plans. See our track plan in the Appendix or you can create your own plan. The photography throughout this book and in the SubTerrain video refer to the track plan found in the Appendix.

SubTerrain is adaptable to any track plan, most scales and any type of track. The examples in this book use rigid sectional track, but SubTerrain works equally well with flexible track.

Once you have selected a suitable plan, transfer it to your base. In most circumstances, a sheet of plywood makes an adequate base. Simply lay out track on base and trace around it or draw on base.

Now you are ready for SubTerrain's five easy steps:

Overview

Install Risers

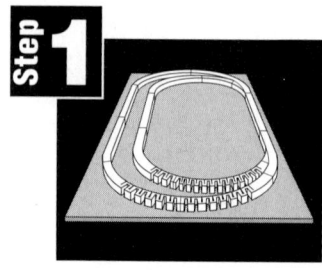 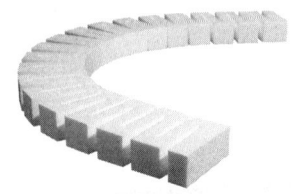

Install Risers wherever track will be laid. This raises the track level to the height of the Risers, causing surrounding areas to be lower. You can quickly and easily make creeks and other low-lying areas without cutting into the layout base. (See page 10)

Add Inclines

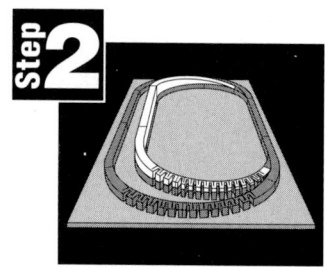 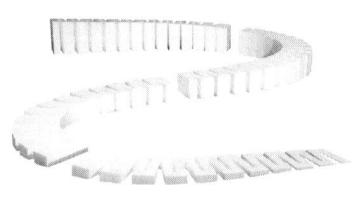

Use flexible Inclines to easily change track elevations on curves or straights. The SubTerrain System's precut Inclines (with 2% or 4% grade) remove the guesswork and complicated calculations. (See page 17)

Install Profile Boards

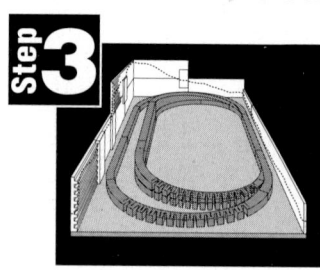 

Install interlocking Profile Boards with matching Connectors to make a sturdy layout perimeter that can easily be cut with the Hot Wire Foam Cutter or a hobby knife to conform to any profile desired. (See page 22)

Overview

Install Foam Sheets

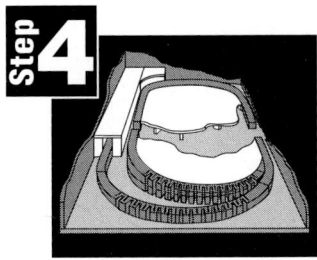 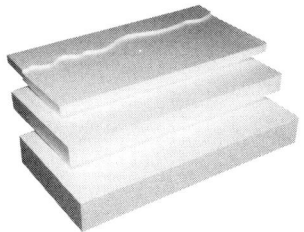

Cut Foam Sheets to enclose tunnels, create interior terrain profiles and form level, elevated areas for buildings and towns. (See page 26)

Add Plaster Cloth and Track-Bed

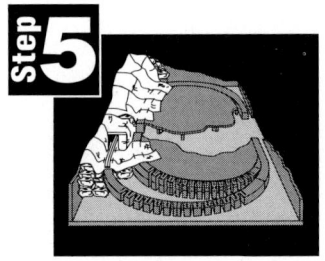 

Form terrain with newspaper wads and cover with Plaster Cloth that has been dipped in water. The Plaster Cloth will dry to a hard shell without adding any plaster. Install the Track-Bed. (See page 32)

Finish Your Layout

Once the SubTerrain base has been created, finish your layout. Lay track. Add streets, roads, curbs, sidewalks and parking lots using the Road System. Add terrain features, landscaping, buildings, structures, people and vehicles. Make the layout realistic and uniquely your own creation. (See page 40)

Before You Begin

A. Select a Plan

SubTerrain allows you to create any layout desired. You can select a plan from a plan book or create one of your own. You can start with a basic track diagram and add features later, or start with a detailed plan which indicates the track position, mountains, rivers, buildings, tunnels, trees and other *terrain* and *landscape* features. The plan featured in this book is located in the Appendix.

B. Select a Base

It is important to have a flat surface for building your layout. SubTerrain is a very versatile system and can be constructed on almost any size or type of base. The 4'x8' plan in this book starts with a sheet of 5/8", grade A/C plywood.

Because SubTerrain is lightweight, the layout can be supported by a table, sawhorses or you can build a stand for it. The important thing is to keep the layout flat during construction. Being lightweight makes SubTerrain ideal for situations where the layout will have to be moved, such as where space is limited or for *modular layouts*.

C. Transfer the Plan to the Base

Once you have a plan and a base, it's time to bring the two together.

The examples in this book use HO *scale* rigid sectional track. You can also use flexible track. The methods for using the SubTerrain System are similar regardless of the type of track or scale you have chosen. See the section Using SubTerrain With Other Scales on page 50.

Assemble and lay track on the base according to your plan. Temporarily pin the track in place with *Foam Nails*. Usually two Foam Nails, one at each

TECH TIP

A simple plywood base is appropriate for most circumstances. Use at least 1/2" to 3/4" grade A/C plywood. Face the best side of the plywood up for a clean, flat surface to support your SubTerrain.

For an unusually large layout, or if you want additional strength, bracing can be added to the bottom of the plywood for additional support.

7

end of a track section, are sufficient. Track sections should be butted tightly together; check joints for a tight fit. Trace a line around both sides of your track directly on the plywood base.

If your detailed plan includes other terrain and landscape features, sketch those in now. This will help clarify the *track plan*, and will ensure all of the details of the plan will work together. If you have not decided where all of your terrain features will go, or they don't appear as part of your plan, you can work them in to fit later.

Foam Pencils come in two colors. Use one color to draw your track outline and another color to sketch in other features of your plan. This will help keep the layout clear.

Trace a line around both sides of your track directly on the plywood base.

Woodland Scenics' Foam Pencils are ideally suited for drawing on a variety of surfaces, including wood and SubTerrain foam products. Some pencils will damage foam; Foam Pencils are soft and will not damage foam. Many markers and other writing products will bleed through paint or other *porous* coverings,  leaving unsightly marks on your landscape. Foam Pencils use a special compound that will not bleed through your layout. Foam Pencils are packaged in two colors so you can mark and distinguish different aspects of your layout.

Look over your layout to be sure there are no obvious problems with the plan. If you spot any problem areas now is the time to correct them. Once you are satisfied with your plan and have it clearly marked on the plywood base, remove the track. Now you are ready to use the SubTerrain System to build your layout.

9

Install Risers

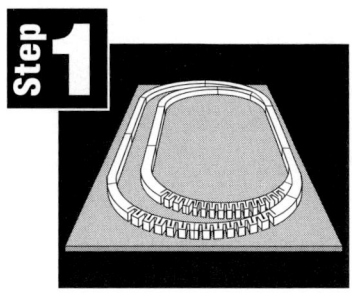

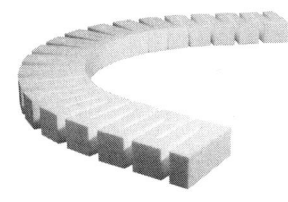

Risers serve as an elevated base for track and roads and are available in 1/2", 1", 2" and 4" heights.

Elevating the track above the base with Risers allows for dramatic scenery possibilities, such as ravines and creeks without the need for cutting into the base.

Without Risers

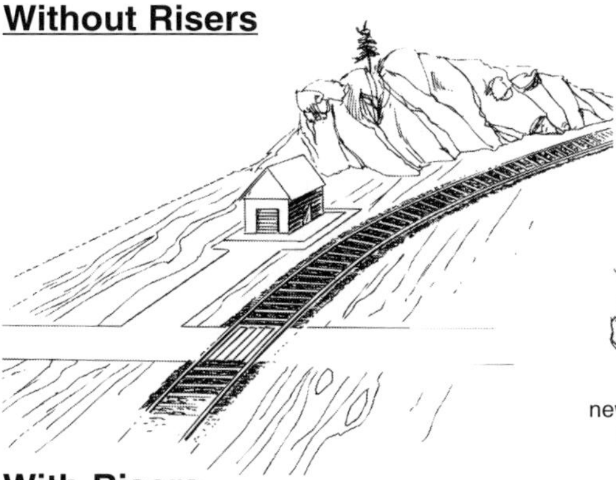

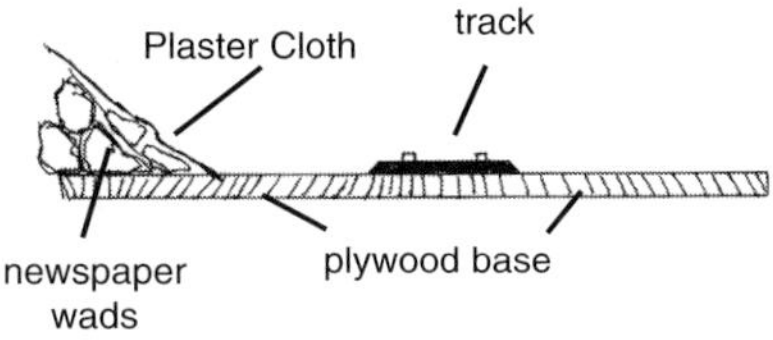

Plaster Cloth   track

newspaper wads   plywood base

With Risers

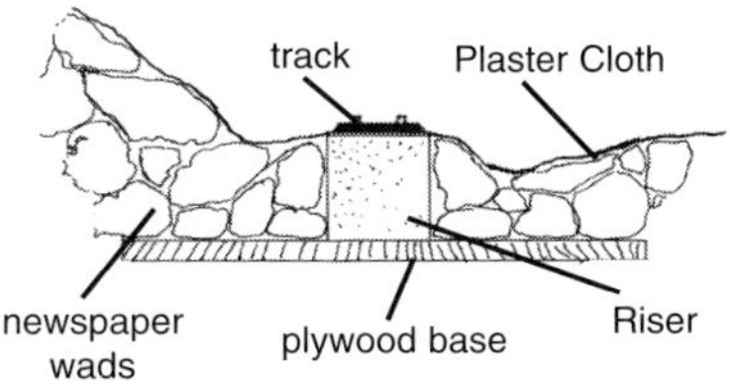

track   Plaster Cloth

newspaper wads   plywood base   Riser

10

A. What Size Do I Need

Use at least 2" Risers to elevate track. This will provide moderate *elevation* for gradual *relief*, hills and creekbeds. For a more dramatic landscape, use 4" Risers to give maximum elevation for steep relief, rivers and valleys. 1/2" and 1" Risers are generally used in conjunction with *Incline Starters*. (See page 19)

B. How Many Risers Do I Need

Risers are two feet long and are sold in packs of two or four, depending upon the height. Risers will be placed under the entire track. Determine the total length of your track in feet. You will need the same number of feet in Risers.

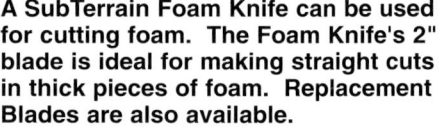

A SubTerrain Foam Knife can be used for cutting foam. The Foam Knife's 2" blade is ideal for making straight cuts in thick pieces of foam. Replacement Blades are also available.

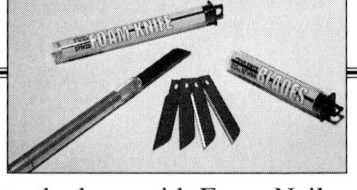

C. Install Risers

Center Risers over the track outline previously drawn on your base. Butt the Riser sections tightly together. Temporarily pin the Risers to the base with Foam Nails. If your plan calls for bridges, leave the correct space between Risers for each bridge. Check the manufacturer's instructions for each bridge or review "Install Bridges" on page 36.

Use Foam Nails to firmly hold Risers in place. Space Foam Nails 8-10" apart on straight sections and outside curves. For tighter inside curves, space Foam Nails 4-6" apart.

Our track plan (see page 67) calls for inner and outer loops that come together along the front of the layout. Your plan may have several such loops and may include crossovers, intersections, *turnouts*, overpasses and other features.

Temporarily pin the Risers to base with Foam Nails.

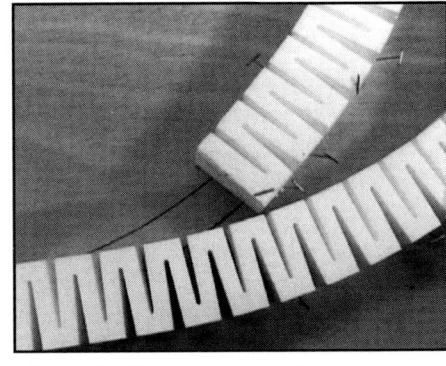

Where the Risers come together at a turnout, there will be a gap that will be filled in later.

On turnouts, install the straight section of Riser first. Then butt the turnout portion tightly against that section. This will leave a triangular gap between the Risers which will be filled in later (See Diverging Risers on page 20).

When cutting Risers, an exact fit is not necessary. Small gaps between Risers will be covered later with *Plaster Cloth* and *Track-Bed* (see page 32). Risers installed around a curve may tend to lift up on the inside edge. Pin these firmly in place with Foam Nails.

When installing SubTerrain, you may have to cut the foam. We recommend the Hot Wire Foam Cutter. This tool was designed to cut SubTerrain's high-density foam quickly and easily. SubTerrain foam is made of expanded polystyrene which emits no toxic fumes when cut with the Hot Wire Foam Cutter. Some other foam products do emit toxic fumes when cut with a Hot Wire Foam Cutter. We recommend using a Hot Wire Foam Cutter only on SubTerrain's white foam products.

Hot Wire Foam Cutter

The optional Bow and Guide make the Hot Wire Foam Cutter even more versatile. The Guide can be used to cut precise angles.

Bow & Guide Attachment

The Hot Wire Foam Cutter is designed to use special *nichrome wire*. Use only Woodland Scenics Replacement Wire with your Hot Wire Foam Cutter.

Gluing and Securing SubTerrain

The SubTerrain System includes two types of glue, each has its own properties and techniques. For best results with SubTerrain we recommend using both types of glue, as each is suited for different applications. However, it is possible to select only one type of glue and use it throughout the entire assembly process. We recommend you read this chapter, and refer back to it as often as necessary while you are gluing SubTerrain products in place.

Woodland Scenics Low Temp Foam Glue Gun is intended for use with SubTerrain foam. The gun's operating temperature will not melt SubTerrain foam, and the special Low Temp Glue Sticks are ideal for fast bonding to foam and wood. Woodland Scenics Low Temp Foam Glue Gun should only be used with our specially formulated Low Temp Glue Sticks. Gun should be preheated for about 5 minutes before using.

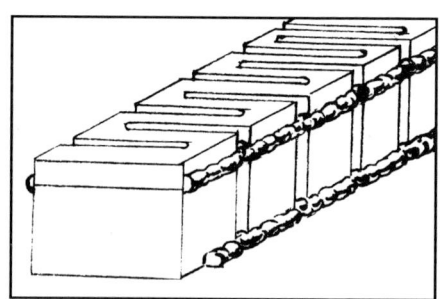

A. Low Temp Foam Glue Gun

Woodland Scenics *Low Temp Foam Glue Gun* is specially designed to work with SubTerrain and other Foam products. The special gun, and the specially formulated *Low Temp Foam Glue* Sticks operate at a lower temperature than ordinary glue guns, so they will not melt SubTerrain foam. The Glue Sticks will bond quickly to wood, foam, cork, Homasote, cloth, and a variety of other products common in modeling and handicrafts.

Run a bead of glue in the seam between two pieces of material.

Use the Low Temp Foam Glue Gun to run a bead of glue along the seam between the two pieces of material, much like you would apply caulk. The glue will set quickly, and it is usually not necessary to move or disassemble your

work in order to apply glue.

It is usually not necessary to move or disassemble your work in order to apply glue.

Using this 'caulking' technique you could hold off on gluing any products together until the entire layout has been assembled and tested. This allows you to make changes as you work, and enables you to put a layout together, test it, refine it, add or remove sections, all before permanently gluing anything in place.

Pin the entire layout together with Foam Nails, then secure everything with the Low Temp Foam Glue Gun when you are satisfied with it.

You can also use the Low Temp Foam Glue between sheets of foam, and between foam and other products. Apply spots of glue to one piece of material, then press the work together. Hold the work in place for a few seconds while the glue sets. The glue will set quickly so work in small areas and apply only a little glue at a time.

Low Temp Foam Glue may cause lumps if it is used underneath thin material such as Track-Bed or the leading edge of an Incline Starter. Use a small piece of cardboard to spread the glue out if necessary prior to pressing your work together. Don't use your fingers to spread this glue. Even though the Low Temp Foam Glue Gun is not as hot as most glue guns, it is still hot enough to burn your skin.

B. Foam Tack Glue

Foam Tack Glue is high-tack and effective on wood, cork, Homasote, rough or smooth hardboard and foam, as well as many other materials commonly used in modeling and handicrafts.

We prefer to use Foam Tack Glue to adhere Risers and Inclines. Foam Tack Glue is high-tack and effective on most materials including foam, wood, cork, Homasote, Upsom board and rough or smooth hardboard. Foam Tack Glue is specially formulated to dry thoroughly. Many white glues will not dry properly between two large foam sheets or on other large surfaces. Foam Tack Glue solves this problem and is ideal for use any time you have two large surfaces to bond.

Foam Tack Glue can also be used as a contact cement, as explained in the Tech-Tip on the following page.

Foam Tack Glue is different from other white glues. It is specially formulated to dry thoroughly. If you've ever used white glue to glue two sheets of foam together, you know that the glue will seldom dry all the way through, and will leave wet spots in the middle of your work. Foam Tack Glue will dry thoroughly.

Foam Tack Glue is especially useful when gluing thin or narrow pieces together. Apply a bead of glue and press work together. Foam Tack Glue sets more slowly than Low Temp Foam Glue. Work will have to be pinned together with Foam Nails, clamped together or weighed down while the glue sets. Drying time will depend upon heat and humidity. When Foam Tack Glue is used as a *contact cement* it will bond instantly. No additional clamping or drying time is needed.

Because Foam Tack Glue must be spread on the surface of the materials to be adhered together you will have to take your work apart in order to apply the glue.

Use Foam Tack Glue underneath the leading edge of an Incline, or other thin material.

If you are using Foam Tack Glue for the entire layout we recommend testing your layout and gluing foam in place after each step. For example, after installing all of your Risers, lay your track on top of the Risers. Be sure the joints between track sections are tight. Be sure your track is centered over the Risers. If necessary unpin and adjust the position of your Risers. Once you are satisfied with the position of your Risers glue them in place. Remove one Riser at a time. Apply a bead of glue to the plywood base beneath the Riser. Press the Riser back in place, and pin it down with Foam Nails until the glue sets.

 TECH TIP

Foam Tack Glue can also be used as a contact cement. Apply a thin coat of Foam Tack Glue to both surfaces to be bonded. Set the pieces aside for a few minutes until the glue is dry to the touch. Place the two glued surfaces together. The Foam Tack Glue will bond instantly. This is the ideal method for installing Track-Bed.

If the Foam Tack Glue is still wet when surfaces are mated, some pinning or clamping may be needed.

Once you have glued down the Risers proceed to Step Two - Add *Inclines*. Repeat this testing and gluing process after each step.

Add Inclines

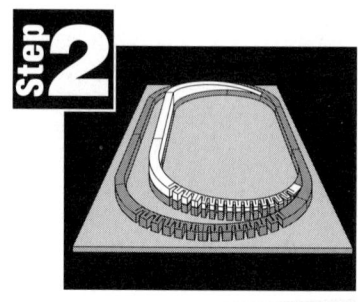 

Inclines support your track as it maneuvers through changes in elevation. Hills, mountains, ravines, creeks and river beds are all a part of the natural terrain that you can model. These terrain features make your layout more interesting and realistic. Inclines allow your train to climb and descend hills as it moves through the landscape.

The SubTerrain System includes *Incline Sets* and Incline Starters in 2% and 4% *grades*. Use them to realistically take your track from one elevation to another, without complicated calculations, guesswork or wood construction. Simply stack the precut, premeasured Inclines on top of the Risers for quick and easy elevation changes.

A. Before Installing Inclines

You need to decide what grade of Incline to use. To determine this, you need to know the elevation from the lowest point on the track to the highest point, and the total track length available between these two points. Now you can determine the grade needed.

CHART TO DETERMINE PERCENT INCLINE						
Desired Elevation from Roadbed:	1"	2"	3"	4"	5"	6"
# feet to reach elevation using:						
2% incline	4'	8'	12'	16'	20'	24'
4% incline	2'	4'	6'	8'	10'	12'

SubTerrain Inclines are available in 2% or 4% grades. They can be used independently or combined to make grades of 6% or more. Using this chart, determine the right grade for your situation. First determine the desired elevation from the lowest to the highest point of your track. Look down that column on the chart and find the minimum track length needed to reach that elevation. Move to the left of that row to determine the grade needed.

In most cases a 4% grade works best in limited space. Some engines will have trouble pulling cars up grades steeper than 4%. Test run your engine with a number of cars to be sure it will pull the grade you select.

When considering total track length available to create an incline, remember that your train must go up the incline and come back down. Since it is possible to climb and descend at two different grades, the chart only considers the distance available for one side of the incline. You should also refer to your layout plan and consider features such as turnouts, bridges and other elements when determining the total track length. Often these features are level, and your track must level out on either side of these features.

We find that a 4% grade is ideal for most situations. Although this is steeper than many real railroads would use, it allows for interesting changes in elevation over a short distance. Although you can use SubTerrain to create grades steeper than 4%, you should check your engine to be certain it will pull a long train up a steep grade.

● *Incline Sets*

SubTerrain Incline Sets include everything necessary to raise the elevation of your track from 0" to 4". This is the ideal elevation for overpasses (in HO scale). Incline Sets come in either 2% or 4% grades. For most track plans and layouts Incline Sets are the ideal way to add elevation to your layout quickly and easily.

2% Incline Set

The 2% Incline Set requires a 16' run to elevate the track 4". This set includes 8 pieces each 24" long.

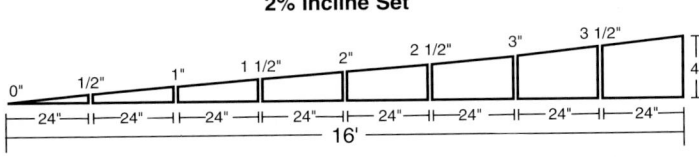

4% Incline Set

The 4% Incline Set requires only an 8' run to elevate the track 4". This set includes 4 pieces each 24" long.

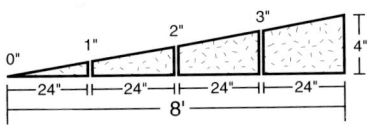

18

● Incline Starters

The SubTerrain System also includes Incline Starters. An Incline Starter is a wedge of high-density foam used to start your track on an Incline. A 2% Incline Starter raises the elevation from 0" to 1/2" over a length of 2 feet. A 4% Incline Starter raises the elevation from 0" to 1" over a length of 2 feet. Incline Starters can be used in stairstep fashion with 1/2" and 1" Risers to raise an incline to any height.

● Stair-step Risers and Inclines

A 2% Incline Starter will elevate the track 1/2". A 4% Incline Starter will elevate the track 1". Incline Starters can be stacked on 1/2" and 1" Risers to continue the incline to a higher elevation. Using a combination of Risers and Inclines in stair-step fashion, you can obtain any elevation.

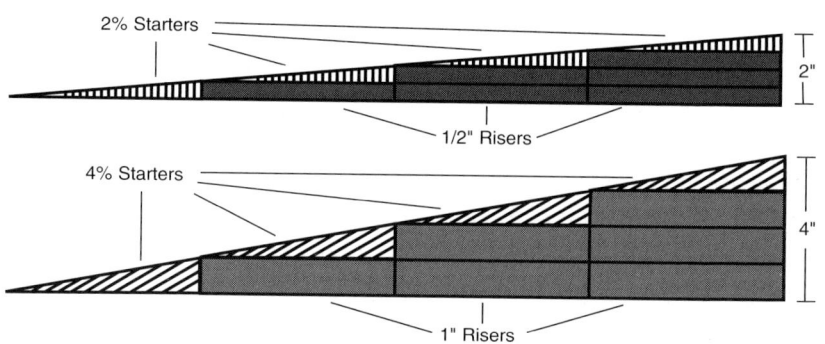

B. Install Inclines

Once you have determined the right SubTerrain Inclines to use, it is time to install them on your layout. Center the Inclines on top of the Risers and pin them in place with Foam Nails.

Center the Inclines on top of the Risers and pin them in place with Foam Nails.

19

As with Risers, you may need to cut Inclines to fit. Use your Hot Wire Foam Cutter or Foam Knife.

● Diverging Risers

If your layout calls for turnouts or intersections, you may have some small gaps to fill. A transition piece can be made with *Foam Sheets.*

This can be accomplished one of two ways. You can cut a solid block of foam to fill the entire gap. This solid piece of foam should be the same height as the Risers. You may also wish to cut a thinner piece of foam and support it underneath with small scraps of foam. Use at least 1" foam for proper support.

A transition piece can be made with a portion of a Riser or scrap foam.

To cut this piece to the proper size slip a piece of paper underneath your Risers at the gap. Trace the outline of the missing wedge on this paper. Transfer this outline to a Foam Sheet. Cut the foam and pin it in place with Foam Nails.

● Test Your Layout

Once all of the Risers and Inclines are in place, you may want to test your track. Lay the track sections directly on top of the SubTerrain foam. Pin track in place using Foam Nails. Put Foam Nails in at an angle or push them all the way in to avoid interfering with your train.

Use *rail joiners* to join the track sections together. Be sure to use insulated rail joiners, where appropriate, to ensure proper wiring and current flow. If you are unsure how to wire the track, follow your track plan or review one of the many books on wiring available from your retailer.

Run wiring neatly down the sides of Risers and Inclines and along the base to the power supply. Connect all necessary wiring to the track, turnouts and the power supply. Follow the wiring instructions for your track plan, power supply and turnouts.

Now you can test run your train. Check for derailing. If you need to make adjustments, Risers and Inclines can be removed and repositioned. Gaps and rough spots may seem to be a problem now but will be smoothed over later with Plaster Cloth (See page 32). This is also a good time to be sure your engine will pull your train up steeper grades. At this point, check Risers and Inclines to be certain they are centered under the track and the track joints all fit together tightly.

 **TECH TIP**

Where an Incline Starter, or the first piece of an Incline Set meets a Riser there may be a small ridge or bump. This is usually not a problem, as it will be smoothed over later with Plaster Cloth (see Step 5). If you are concerned about this you can fill this gap with Foam Putty.

Apply Foam Putty after the Risers and Inclines have been glued in place. Foam Putty can be sculpted when applied, or sanded when dry. Use 220 grit sandpaper for rough sanding. Finish with 320 grit.

The best way to achieve a smooth edge when sanding is to make a sanding block slightly wider than the width of your Risers. Sand lengthwise along the top of the Risers and Inclines. Use long smooth strokes, and apply very little pressure.

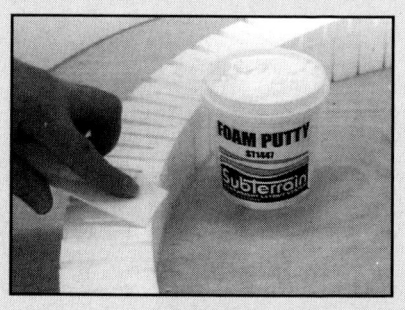

 Foam Putty is a non-shrinking, very lightweight filling material with the same characteristics as foam. Foam Putty requires no mixing and dries a bright white color. It may be used to fill cracks between foam pieces, gaps and holes in the layout. It can be sculpted when wet and sanded or carved when dry.

Cut & Install Profile Boards

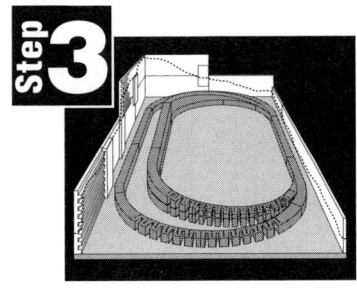

Profile Boards are used around the perimeter of the layout. They support the terrain surface that you will create later. *Connectors* come with Profile Boards and are used to lock the Profile Boards together for a secure assembly. The special design of Profile Boards and Connectors allow them to interlock, making a strong assembly both horizontally and vertically, even before gluing. Profile Boards can be stacked and locked together with Connectors to reach almost any height. Profile Boards are 24" long and 8" tall. Each package contains 2 Profile Boards and 2 Connectors.

 TECH TIP

Profile Boards and Connectors are molded to fit together very tightly for extra stability. Avoid indenting foam with your fingers while connecting Profile Boards by placing a scrap piece of foam between your hand and the Profile Board. If no scrap foam is available use any flat object, such as a book.

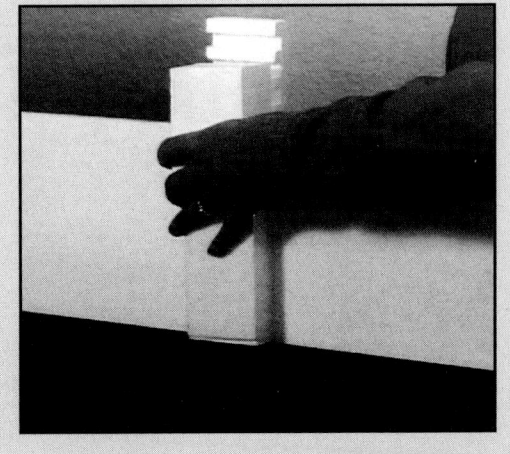

A. Place the First Row of Profile Boards Around the Perimeter of the Layout.

Join sections together with Connectors. Profile Boards are designed to interlock at corners by turning one board upside down. Pin the Profile Boards to the base with Foam Nails.

For a seamless joint, the Profile Boards can be cut at a 45° angle (*mitered*) at the corner using the Hot Wire Foam Cutter with Guide attachment.

Profile Boards are designed to interlock at corners.

Profile Boards may extend past the end of the base. If this happens trim the end of the profile board with the Hot Wire Foam Cutter or Foam Knife. Use a straight edge to ensure a straight, square cut.

Where higher elevations are required, additional Profile Boards can be added. Stack these above the first row of Profile Boards and join with Connectors.

> **TECH TIP**
>
> **If you run out of Connectors you can create your own. Simply cut 3" from the end of a Profile Board. Use this 3" section as a Connector.**

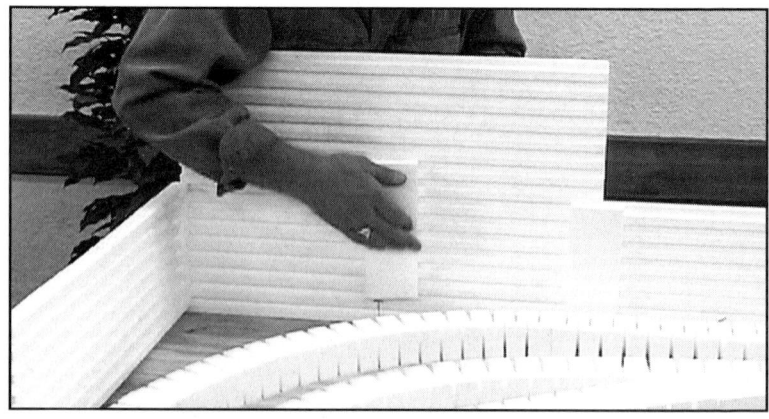

For higher elevations, additional Profile Boards may be added by stacking above first row and joining with Connectors.

23

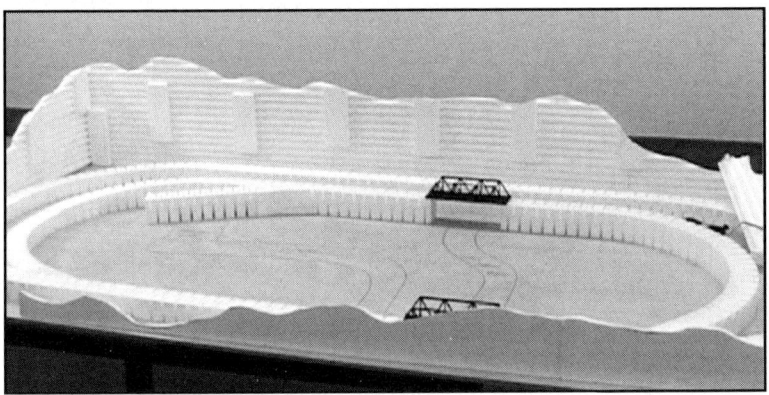

Profile Boards can be cut with the Hot Wire Foam Cutter or hobby knife to create contours around the perimeter of your layout.

B. Cut Contours

Profile Boards can now be cut to create the contours around the perimeter of your layout. If your track plan provides a pattern for the exterior profile, or you know approximately what you want this profile to look like, you can cut it now. If you are not sure what contours you want, wait until after you have created your interior terrain features with paper wads. (See page 32.)

To cut the profile's contour, first draw the contour on the outside of the Profile

 **TECH TIP**

Profile Boards can be easily cut with the Hot Wire Foam Cutter. The optional Bow attachment can be used for a more ergonomic cutting angle.

Use a sawing motion with the wire for a faster cut.

Boards with a Foam Pencil. Then use the Hot Wire Foam Cutter to cut along the drawn line. If you make a mistake or don't like the contours you have created, simply re-attach the pieces of Profile Boards with the Low Temp Foam Glue Gun.
Wipe off excess glue.

Later you will cover the perimeter of your layout with Plaster Cloth, covering any seams or gaps in the Profile Boards. This will create a hard surface to protect your perimeter walls and hide seams, gaps and imperfections in the exterior.

 **TECH TIP**

To save material, you may wish to turn the cut-off pieces upside down for use in the front of your layout or in areas where the profile is lower. These cut-off pieces can also be stacked on the top edge of other Profile Boards.

The exterior or flat side of Profile Boards has raised marks from the molding process. If you wish, sand these out with a 320 grit sandpaper. Use a sanding block for a smooth finish.

Permanently glue the Profile Boards and Connectors to each other and to the base. The Hot Wire Foam Cutter will cut through Low Temp Foam Glue.

Install Foam Sheets

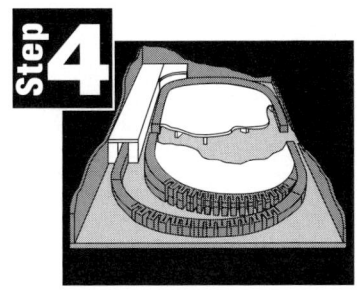

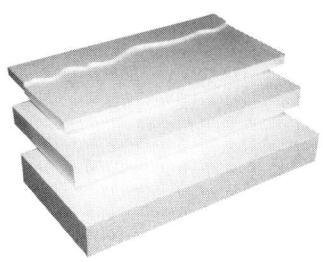

Sheet goods are made from the same nontoxic, high-density foam that is used for the entire SubTerrain System. Foam Sheets are available in 1/4", 1/2", 1", 2", 3" and 4" thicknesses.

These sheets are ideal for creating elevated, flat areas for towns, tunnel walls and ceilings and contour supports. The 1/4" and 1/2" sheets can be bent to almost any radius.

Woodland Scenics SubTerrain white foam does not emit hazardous fumes when cut with a hot wire cutter. Our foam is high density, expanded polystyrene which is nontoxic and does not damage the ozone layer.

Foam insulation boards (sold in most lumberyards) are usually made with extruded polystyrene foam and emit low levels of toxic fumes when cut with a hot wire cutter. This should only be done with good ventilation. Many extruded polystyrene products also use ozone depleting chemicals.

Polyurethane foam; rigid and flexible (foam rubber) emits extremely toxic fumes if cut with a hot wire cutter. Polyurethane foam should never be cut with a hot wire cutter.

Our white foam is perfectly safe to cut with a hot wire cutter; obviously some foam is not safe. We recommend our Hot Wire Foam Cutter be used only on expanded polystyrene -- like SubTerrain's white foam products. Anyone allergic to any kind of smoke should use good ventilation, even when cutting our white foam.

A. Create Level Elevated Areas

When creating towns, parking areas or placing buildings you might want an elevated flat area. Don't worry about actually elevating the area yet; simply decide where the area will be located and what shape it should be. Free span level areas should use at least 1" thick foam. If the elevated area must fit the contours of a Riser or other feature, trace the contour on a sheet of paper; then transfer the shape to a sheet of foam. Cut the contour with a Hot Wire Foam Cutter or Foam Knife.

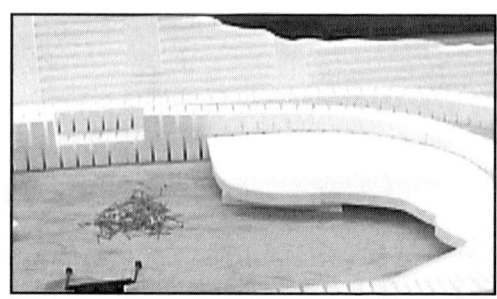

Use at least a 1" Foam Sheet for elevated areas.

To support the elevated areas, cut several small pieces of foam to the proper height. These pieces can be cut from scraps of foam left over from previous operations. Pin the foam in place to test the height of your supports. When you are satisfied with the fit and support, glue the foam down with the Low Temp Foam Glue Gun or Foam Tack Glue.

B. Create Tunnels

You can also cut Foam Sheets to form tunnel sides and ceilings. These will support terrain contours and keep the track area clear. Pin the foam in place with Foam Nails and check for clearance.

To ensure adequate clearance between tunnel sides and track, space the walls at least 1/2" from the Risers. You can use scrap pieces of 1/2" foam as spacers. For curved tunnel walls, use 1/4" foam and bend to fit.

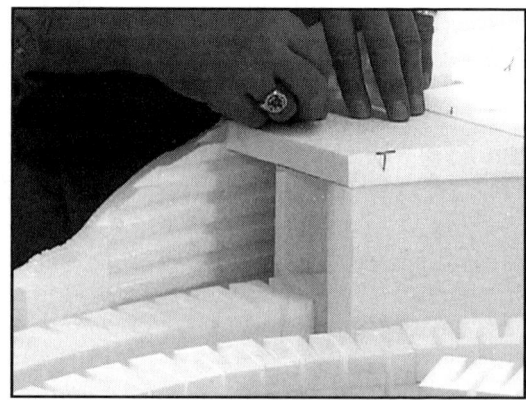

Foam Sheets may be used to form tunnel walls and ceilings.

27

(See Create Vertical Curved Areas on page 29.)

Before permanently attaching the tunnel sides and ceiling, you will need to install the track in areas covered by the tunnel. In these areas, create a Plaster Cloth *hardshell*; then install the Track-Bed and finally the track. These steps are covered in more detail later.

The easiest way to create a realistic tunnel floor is to glue the walls in place, then lay Plaster Cloth between the walls and on top of the Risers. Put wads of newspaper between Riser and tunnel walls to support Plaster Cloth, if necessary. Now lay the Track-Bed and track. Refer to Step 5 on page 32 for help on using Plaster Cloth and laying Track-Bed. Refer to Finishing Your Layout on page 40 for help on laying track.

Once the track has been installed, glue the ceiling in place with the Low Temp Foam Glue Gun.

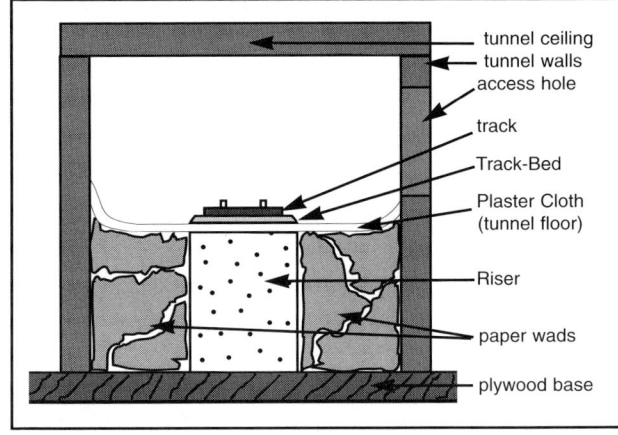

tunnel ceiling
tunnel walls
access hole
track
Track-Bed
Plaster Cloth (tunnel floor)
Riser
paper wads
plywood base

Put newspaper wads between Risers and tunnel walls to support Plaster Cloth.

🏵 **TECH TIP**

Remember you will have Plaster Cloth and Track-Bed between the foam and the track, so you will need to allow for that when checking the clearance for the tunnel ceiling.

🏵 **TECH TIP**

If your layout calls for tunnels or other hard to reach areas, cut *access holes* in the Profile Boards with a Foam Knife. If the train derails in this area, you can now reach it easily.

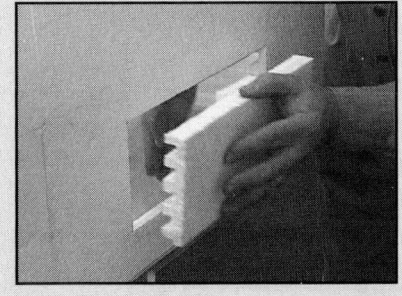

C. Create Vertical Curved Areas

If your tunnel curves, you will need to bend the tunnel wall, creating a vertical curved area. Vertical curved areas can also be used to support flat areas and create bluff faces or *retaining walls*.

Cut a sheet of 1/4" or 1/2" foam to the desired height. Gently flex the foam back and forth. You will hear it "give" as you flex it. Pin the foam in place with Foam Nails. Once the foam is positioned correctly, you can glue it in place with the Low Temp Foam Glue Gun (or other glue).

After flexing, 1/4" Foam Sheets work great for curves. Pin in place with Foam Nails and glue in place with the Low Temp Foam Glue Gun.

D. Build Streets and Roads

Roads may rise and fall faster and turn and bank more sharply than tracks; therefore they can be fit in almost anywhere. You will need streets and roads to the industries, towns and other buildings on your layout. Since the roads on your layout bear no significant weight, they may be suspended (as shown) and supported periodically with pieces of scrap foam. Later, streets and roads will be covered with Plaster Cloth and paved with the Woodland Scenics Road System.

To build roads, use any combination of Risers and Incline Sets and Starters in the same manner as they were used to support your track. Roads are generally wider than railroad track so you may need to place two Risers side-by-side to support the road.

Pin Risers and Inclines in place with Foam Nails. Once you are satisfied with the position of your roads, glue

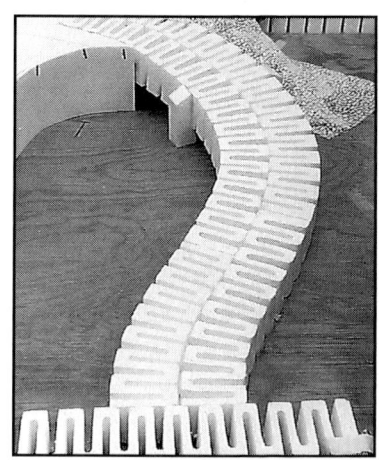

Roads are generally wider than railroad track so two Risers may be placed side-by-side to create a road. Notice in the foreground that the road is the same level as the track, and rises to the elevated areas.

the foam in place with the Low Temp Foam Glue Gun.

E. Make Contour Supports

For extra support and to help you visualize how the terrain will flow, use Foam Sheets as contour supports. You can use scrap pieces left over from previous steps. Use the Hot

Cut contour supports out of scrap foam with the Hot Wire Foam Cutter or Foam Knife.

Wire Foam Cutter or Foam Knife to cut foam pieces to the shape you desire. Glue supports in place with the Low Temp Foam Glue Gun.

F. Install Wiring

Before creating a Plaster Cloth hardshell you should install wiring. Installing wiring is simple and fast with SubTerrain. Run wire along, and if necessary through, Risers and Inclines to connect the track to the power supply and switch control boxes to electric switches.

Locate wiring positions on turnouts and track. Leave about 3" of wire unattached and temporarily tape over the exposed ends.

 **TECH TIP**

Toggle switches can be mounted in your Profile Boards. Cut a hole in your Profile Board with the Foam Knife, or use a drill. Install the toggle switch just as you would in hardboard. Use a fender washer for extra support. Wire appropriately.

Make a hole in the foam just large enough for the wire, or run wire down the sides and along Risers and Inclines. Tack wire in place with the Low Temp Foam Glue Gun. Make one exit for a neater appearance.

If you prefer, drill a hole through the Inclines, Risers and the plywood base. This hole should be just large enough for your wire to pass through. On the underside of the layout, route the wiring to your power supply or electric switches. If you plan on building a table for your layout, be certain it will not interfere with the wiring.

Use *Cable ties* (*zip ties*) to bundle wires together to keep them neat. Cable ties are available in most electronic stores.

Try not to place wiring joints in areas that will be covered by the Plaster Cloth hardshell, as these will be difficult to service later. Use continuous wiring runs wherever possible. If it is necessary to join wires, be sure to solder them carefully to provide a good mechanical and electrical joint. Be sure to follow the safety instructions for your soldering iron or gun, and be careful not to melt SubTerrain foam while soldering.

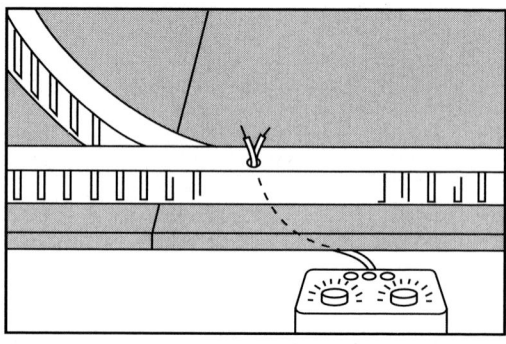

Drill hole through Incline, Risers and plywood base for your wiring.

For a cleaner appearance to your layout we recommend you run all of your wiring underneath the Plaster Cloth hardshell to a single exit point, where you can make all of your final connections.

TECH TIP

We recommend hiding all of your wiring underneath the Plaster Cloth hardshell. Run your wiring along the top of the layout to a single exit point along the perimeter. Make your final connections to power supplies or other devices here. All of your wiring will be covered over with Plaster Cloth in Step 5.

Once all SubTerrain foam is in place you are ready to add terrain contours with Plaster Cloth.

Add Plaster Cloth & Track-Bed

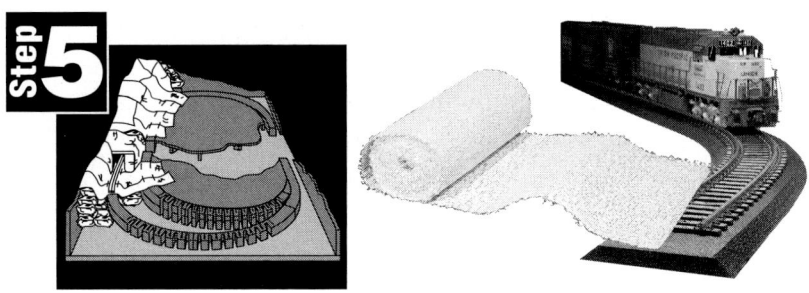

Woodland Scenics Plaster Cloth is a plaster-coated cloth for terrain modeling. Plaster Cloth, when dipped in water, is used to form a hard terrain shell (hardshell), without adding plaster. It easily accepts coloring, rock castings and landscape materials.

A. Create Terrain Contours

Before creating the hardshell, fill in terrain contours with paper wads.

Wad up sheets of newspaper and stack them on the layout between and around contour supports to form the shape of mountains, hills and land contours. Make your wads in a pillow shape by

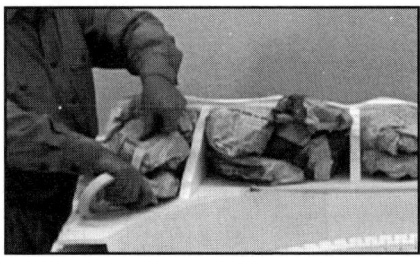

When you are satisfied with your layout contours, use masking tape to hold paper wads in place.

🌳 TECH TIP

When making newspaper wads for terrain building, the best shape for the wads is a pillow shape. Start with a sheet of newspaper and roll the edges underneath from each side until a small pillow with a gently curved top, slightly concave bottom and rounded edges is achieved. These pillow shaped newspaper wads will be easier to stack up than wads of miscellaneous shapes to form the terrain contours.

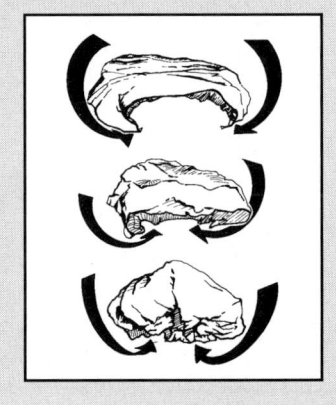

32

rolling the edges underneath from each side. The pillow should have a gently curved top, slightly concave bottom, and rounded edges. This will allow the pillows to fit together neatly and provide a smooth upper surface for laying Plaster Cloth.

🌀 TECH TIP

If you have trouble seeing these mounds as terrain features, place a sheet of newspaper over the paper wads and mist with water. The newspaper will conform to the created shape and provide a better idea of how the contours will look.

Be sure to consider the clearance needs of your trains when you lay out your contours.

Move the newspaper wads around to experiment with contours in different areas. Use masking tape to hold the paper wads in place when you achieve a satisfactory appearance.

B. Make a Hardshell

If you have not done so already, now is the time to cut the terrain contours in your Profile Boards. Refer to "Cut Contours" on page 24 for this step.

Covering the layout with Plaster Cloth will provide a smooth, self-supporting hardshell. On this surface you will mount Track-Bed and track. Then add *rock outcroppings*, *tunnel portals*, retaining walls, landscaping materials, buildings and other features.

Cut the Plaster Cloth in strips of manageable size, usually 8-18 inches is easiest to work with. One side of the Plaster Cloth is bumpy because it has a heavier coat of plaster. Apply Plaster Cloth with the bumpy side up to more easily smooth the plaster and optimize strength.

While the Plaster Cloth is still wet, use your hands to fill in holes and smooth.

Dip a strip of Plaster Cloth in water and lay it on the paper wads. Plaster Cloth will conform to the shape of the underlying material. While it is still wet, rub the Plaster Cloth with your hands to fill holes in the cloth and smooth it out.

Where Plaster Cloth meets the tops of the Profile Boards or the edge of the plywood base, fold the Plaster Cloth over itself to form a smooth edge. Rub the Plaster Cloth with your hands, pressing firmly. If the Plaster Cloth pulls away from the edge, pin it in place with Foam Nails until it dries. Lay a second sheet of Plaster Cloth in the same manner as the first. Overlap the Plaster Cloth so that 50% of the new piece covers

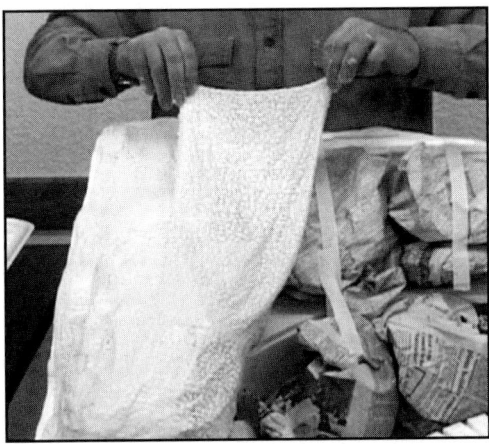

Overlap the Plaster Cloth so that 50% of the new piece covers the previous piece and 50% covers new territory.

the previous piece and 50% covers new territory. Cut strips of Plaster Cloth in half lengthwise and place on both ends of the layout. When applied in this manner you will have two layers of Plaster Cloth over the entire layout, with no overlapping seams. This will produce a very strong covering for your layout, without requiring additional plaster or other bonding materials.

Plaster Cloth should be smooth underneath the track and Track-Bed. Use your hands to smooth these areas while the Plaster Cloth is still wet. The Plaster Cloth will dry hard and firm. After drying it can be sanded to remove any rough spots that remain. Drying time will depend upon heat and humidity.

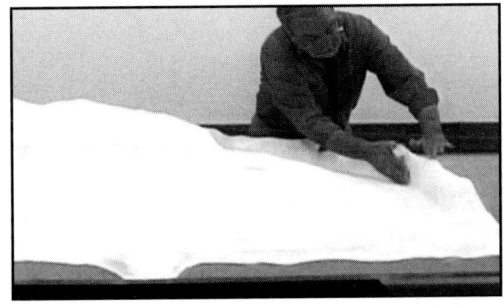

Plaster Cloth forms a hardshell over your entire layout.

C. Cover Perimeter

You can also use Plaster Cloth to create a hardshell on the exterior surface of the Profile Boards. This will increase the strength of your layout, and also provide a clean, smooth surface for painting. In order to prevent seams from showing, the Plaster Cloth on the exterior should be butted together rather than overlapped. Plaster Cloth has scalloped edges. Be sure to cut these off with scissors or Foam Knife when butting Plaster Cloth edge-to-edge.

TECH TIP

When the Plaster Cloth is dry you might want to sand the Riser/Incline area smooth. If you are using Woodland Scenics Track-Bed this will not be necessary. Track- Bed is resilient and will compensate for these rough spots, and your train will run smoothly. If you wish to smooth this area out you may fill gaps or rough spots with Smooth-It. When Plaster Cloth and filling products are dry, sand with 120 grit sandpaper then finish with 220 grit. Lightly wipe the sanded area with clean damp cloth after each sanding .

Beginning at the bottom edge of the Profile Board, use Foam Nails to pin a row of dry Plaster Cloth around the outside perimeter of the layout. Do not overlap this Plaster Cloth; butt the ends together. Where elevation around the outside edge is higher, add additional rows of Plaster Cloth.

Plaster Cloth can be used to create a hardshell on the exterior surface of the Profile Boards.

When the Plaster Cloth is pinned in place, use a spray bottle to spray water on the Plaster Cloth. Wet one area at a time, smooth it with your hands and move on. When smoothing the Plaster Cloth, rub the plaster into the holes in the cloth, and blend the seams together for a seamless appearance.

At the top of your layout trim the Plaster Cloth to about an inch above the perimeter and fold this over the top of your layout. Blend this into the hardshell covering your layout. This will provide a smooth upper edge, and strengthen your layout.

If desired for additional strength, add a second layer of Plaster Cloth around the perimeter of your layout. Avoid overlapping the seams where possible. Spray and smooth as before. If seams appear where Plaster Cloth was butted together, they can be filled and smoothed with *Smooth-It*.

Joints may be sanded for smoother finish. Make one light pass with 220 grit sandpaper, then another with 320 grit sandpaper. Use a damp, clean cloth to remove dust between sandings.

The Plaster Cloth perimeter can be painted with latex paint. Flat paint in dark colors gives the best appearance. We recommend painting the perimeter after all scenery and landscaping is in place.

D. Install Bridges

Timing the installation of a bridge depends upon its construction. If your bridge includes a track section as part of the bridge, follow the general guidelines below for adhering the bridge but install it when you install the track. If your bridge has a flat deck on which track will be laid, it should be installed along with Track-Bed.

Bridges differ from manufacturer to manufacturer and between models from the same manufacturer. Review the manufacturer's instructions for your particular bridge. The following instructions may vary slightly for

 **TECH TIP**

If you are concerned with getting an extremely smooth surface below your Track-Bed, Plaster Cloth can be laid on Risers and Inclines separately. Cover all Risers and Inclines with a single layer of dry Plaster Cloth. Where edges meet over a Riser butt them together rather than overlapping. Once all of this Plaster Cloth is in place spray it with water or brush it with a clean wet paint brush. Work in small sections and smooth this Plaster Cloth with your hands. Blend the plaster together at the seams for a seamless finish.

Once this is done create the rest of the hardshell. Cut strips of Plaster Cloth, dip it in water, and cover the rest of the layout. Where Plaster Cloth comes near Risers fold it over or under itself to avoid getting additional Plaster Cloth on the Risers.

your bridge and layout. The bridge should be painted prior to installation.

Some bridges have a thinner or narrower area where the bridge is to be attached to the layout. Examine the underside of your bridge. Use a Foam Pencil to mark your layout where the bridge will rest.

Bridges differ between manufacturer and models. Review the manufacturer's instructions for installing your bridge.

Match elevation of bridge to track on layout.

Double check the bridges position and alignment. Check to be sure it is at the right elevation to meet your track, and also is positioned correctly side to side. Use *shims* or trim away foam wherever necessary to make sure the bridge is placed correctly. When you are satisfied with the position, glue the bridge in place.

E. Lay Track-Bed

Roadbed is used in model railroading for a number of reasons. In real railroads a roadbed, usually made of rocks, would be built up below the tracks. This would provide support for the tracks and train and also would be graded for smooth operation.

In model railroading roadbed is usually installed under the track to take the place of the roadbed used in real railroads. Roadbed should provide support for the track, smooth out any imperfections in the underlying surface, absorb engine and wheel noise and absorb vibrations for more stable and realistic operation. Cork, homasote and foam are the most common products to use for roadbed on model railroads. We think Woodland Scenics Track-Bed is the best choice for roadbed, because it surpasses both cork and homasote in meeting all of the requirements listed above. Track-Bed meets all applicable *NMRA* standards for roadbed.

Track-Bed deadens the sound of your train for quieter operation. It provides for smoother operation and cushions vibrations. Track-Bed is

easier to use than other roadbed products. It can be glued or tacked in place, it does not require pre-soaking, and will not dry out or crumble. Track-Bed is so flexible it can be directly installed in most turns without splitting.

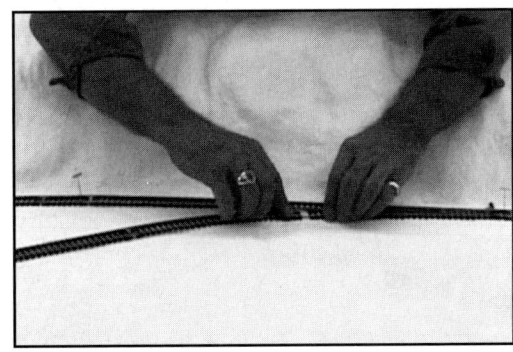

Track-Bed is Woodland Scenics revolutionary roadbed product. Track-Bed is superior to all other forms of roadbed. Track-Bed is highly resilient. It absorbs noise, vibration and irregularities in the underlying base.

Track-Bed has been certified by the NMRA as meeting all applicable standards for roadbed. Track-Bed is easy to cut and install. It is highly flexible and does not require pre-soaking. It will not break, crumble or dry out.

Track-Bed is available in individual strips or in packages of 12 and 36.

Track-Bed can be secured with Foam Tack Glue, Low Temp Foam Glue or it can be tacked. Track-Bed should not be cut with any hot wire cutter. Use a Foam Knife for easy cutting.

Before laying Track-Bed, it is necessary to determine where to put it. Lay track on top of the Plaster Cloth, temporarily pinning it in place with Foam Nails. Temporarily attach wiring and test the track. Check for clearances and derailing.

For clearance, run your longest car all the way around the track in both directions, and check the outside rear corner of the car around curves. When checking for derailing

Temporarily attach wiring and test the track for clearance and derailing.

problems you should run the train both directions around the track. If track joints are uneven, derailing may occur only in one direction. If rough spots seem to be causing a problem you can sand your hardshell, however the Track-Bed will probably correct most of these problems. Other roadbed products are not as resilient, and may actually make

these rough areas worse. If you want to sand the hardshell smooth make one pass with 120 grit sandpaper then follow with 220 grit. Wipe the area with a damp cloth after each sanding to remove dust.

When you are satisfied with the position and operation of the track, trace its outline onto the Plaster Cloth hardshell. Now remove the track.

Use the outline you've just drawn as a guide for laying Track-Bed. Lay it with the narrow or *beveled* side up. Track-Bed is extremely resilient and will conform to very tight curves. Track-Bed is slit down the middle, and can be split apart and laid in two sections for extremely tight curves.

🍂 TECH TIP

Plaster Cloth is a porous material. If excessive moisture gets underneath your Track-Bed the plaster may loosen and the track may lift up. This can be avoided by sealing the Plaster Cloth with Flex Paste. This will create a non-porous surface. Use this technique any place where you feel the Plaster Cloth hardshell will be directly exposed to water.

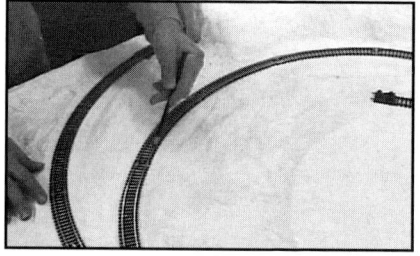

When satisfied with position of track, trace outline onto the Plaster Cloth hardshell.

The best way to apply Track-Bed is to glue it in place with Foam Tack Glue. Spread a thin layer of Foam Tack Glue on the Track-Bed and on the hardshell. Pin the Track-Bed in place while the glue dries. You can also use Foam Tack Glue as a contact cement. Spread a thin layer of Foam Tack Glue on both surfaces. Allow to dry. Press the Track-Bed in place. Glue will bond instantly.

You can also run a bead of Low Temp Foam Glue on the hardshell where Track-Bed will be installed. Spread the glue out before laying Track-Bed; do not use your hands, as Low Temp Foam Glue is still hot enough to burn you. Work in small sections because Low Temp Foam Glue sets quickly.

Run a bead of Woodland Scenics Foam Tack Glue on the hardshell and on back of Track-Bed. Allow to dry. Press Track-Bed in place.

Finishing your Layout

A. Installing Track

Assemble and wire your track according to the track plan. Be sure to review the manufacturer's instructions for installing your track and rail joiners. Test track before gluing it in place.

It might be necessary to remove a small sliver of Track-Bed underneath the *throwbars* of turnouts. This will vary for different track manufacturers. Check the operation of your track. If necessary cut away a small piece of Track-Bed with a hobby knife.

Run a small bead of Foam Tack Glue along the top of Track-Bed and spread it out. For turnouts, be sure not to apply glue to moving parts. Place the track on the Track-Bed and pin it in place until the glue sets. You may wish to weight the track down until the glue dries. Excess Foam Tack Glue can be cleaned with a clean, damp cloth before the glue sets.

B. Using the Road System

Woodland Scenics *Paving Tape*, Smooth-it, *Asphalt Top Coat* and *Concrete Top Coat* are the ideal products for creating highly realistic roads, streets, highways, parking lots, sidewalks and other paved areas. These products are designed to be used directly on top of a Plaster Cloth hardshell but will also work on almost any clean, hard surface.

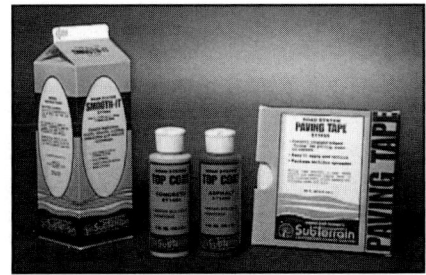

Use Woodland Scenics Paving Tape and Smooth-It with an Asphalt or Concrete Top Coat for any paved area.

Draw road outlines with a Foam Pencil. Keep in mind the scale you are using. A 22' wide road would be 3" wide on an HO scale layout or approximately 1 3/4" wide on an N scale layout. When planning and drawing your roads, include the width of sidewalks and curbs in the overall road width.

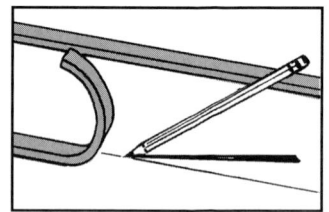

Use our Foam Pencils to draw outlines of roads before laying Paving Tape.

Evenly spread and level Foam Smooth-It between the strips of Paving Tape.

After drawing roads, lay Paving Tape along road edges and press it down firmly. Mix a batch of Smooth-It according to package directions. Use the spreader included with the Paving Tape to evenly spread and level Smooth-It between the strips of Paving Tape. Drying time for Smooth-It will vary depending upon temperature and humidity. Smooth-It should be dry to the touch within 20-30 minutes, longer in more humid areas.

If you are building sidewalks and curbs, add those before removing Paving Tape.

For sidewalks and curbs, lay a strip of Paving Tape over the existing strip or strips beside the road you've just created.

For sidewalks and curbs, lay strips of Paving Tape on existing tape and paved area. Spread Smooth-It between these strips.

Allow Smooth-It to dry one hour before laying paving tape on top. Lay another piece of paving tape on top of the paved area, leaving a gap wide enough for the sidewalk or

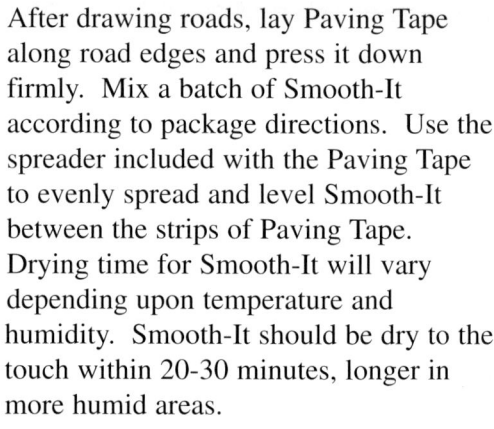

 **TECH TIP**

For a smoother finish on your roads mist Smooth-It lightly with water before it dries.

curb. Spread Smooth-It in the area(s) between these strips of Paving Tape. Allow Smooth-It to dry 20-30 minutes.

Carefully pull Paving Tape away from Smooth-It. Do not leave Paving Tape in place any longer than necessary. When Smooth-It is thoroughly dried, it can be sanded with 220 grit sandpaper.

Once the Smooth-It has dried and been sanded it can be painted with Asphalt or Concrete Top Coat. Then the road can be weathered (see section on page 43).

Carefully pull Paving Tape away from Foam Smooth It.

C. Making Shoulders on a Road

Road shoulders can be created using Fine *Ballast*. Spread a layer of Ballast along the road side. Mist the Ballast with water using a spray bottle. Drip Scenic Cement onto the Ballast with an eye-dropper. Misting the Ballast with water will help the Scenic Cement soak in and blend better with the Ballast. Be sure to spray on enough water to allow the Scenic Cement to flow evenly throughout the Ballast. Once Scenic Cement has dried apply a second coat to ensure thorough coverage.

You can also affix the Ballast in place by misting it with Scenic Cement from a spray bottle. When doing this avoid getting Scenic Cement on the road's surface by masking it off prior to spraying.

For more information on using Ballast and Scenic Cement see Ballast the Track on page 64.

🍃 TECH TIP

If Paving Tape can not be removed easily dampen it lightly with water. Allow water to soak in for a few minutes. Now Paving Tape should come up easily.

🍃 TECH TIP

Cut a scrap of foam to the width desired for your roads and tape a Foam Pencil to each side. Use this tool to trace the outline for all of your roads. This will keep your roads a uniform width.

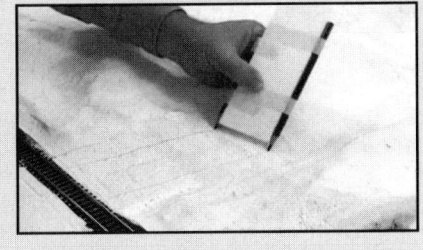

D. Weathering Pavement

Several techniques can be used for weathering pavement. Try one or more of these for a realistic effect.

1. Lightly sand Top Coat with 220 grit sandpaper. This will alter the color and leave streaks and scratches, simulating road wear. Fold the sandpaper to the width of a single lane and sand the road one lane at a time.

2. Blend a small amount of Asphalt and Concrete Top Coats to make different colors. Use a *dry brush* technique to dab spots or streaks of blended Top Coat onto a road already painted (and dry) with normal Top Coat. Use a blend of 10% Concrete Top Coat with 90% Asphalt Top Coat for the best color. You may also experiment with mixing Top Coats in other blends for different color effects. This should give the appearance of skid marks or oil puddles. You don't need to be an artist; the more random and blotchy these areas look, the more realistic they will be.

> Smooth-It can be painted with Asphalt or Concrete Top Coat. These Top Coats are specially formulated for use on any material. They can be used full strength or thinned. Brush Top Coat directly on any smooth, clean surface. Use Top Coats to touch up roads on existing layouts. Thin or clean with water.

3. Thin Top Coat with water. Use thinned Top Coat to paint road surface. This will give a

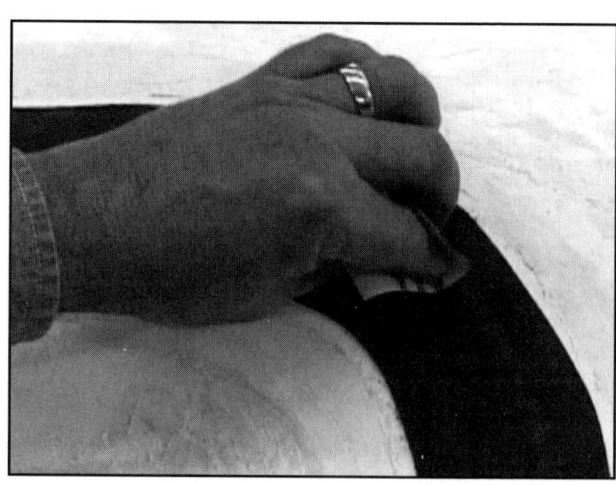

For streaks and scratches, use 220 grit sandpaper.

43

mottled appearance. Blot this on with a wadded rag or sponge.

4. Draw cracks in the pavement with a sharp pencil. Again, don't try to be a perfectionist, just draw in a jagged line for a natural look.

5. There are several ways to add lane markers and stripes to roads and parking lots. We prefer to use a ruling pen, available from most art or office supply stores, with thinned white or yellow paint.

You can use striping tape, also available from art or office supply stores. This tape works very well when applied in straight, or relatively straight areas, but may not work well around curves.

You can also mask off the road around the stripes, then apply white or yellow water based paint. Finish the road first with Asphalt or Concrete Top Coat and allow this to dry thoroughly before applying masking tape. Remove masking tape carefully after the striping paint has dried.

6. Make expansion joints in sidewalks or roads by scoring the dry Smooth-It with a sharp knife.

7. Rub a graphite pencil on coarse (80 grit) sandpaper to produce powdered graphite. With your finger rub this graphite on your sidewalks for natural looking wear.

There is more information on using the Woodland Scenics Road System on page 48. The Road System products can be used on a new layout, or to improve the appearance of roads on an existing layout.

Special Situations

A. More Ideas for Inclines

SubTerrain is extremely versatile and allows you to easily create a base for track in almost any situation. This section contains examples of many special situations you can model using a combination of Risers and Inclines. You will find many more uses for SubTerrain foam as you work and experiment with it.

Incline Sets are specifically designed to raise the elevation of your track 4". On an HO scale layout this is the ideal elevation for overpasses. If you wish to raise to an elevation other than 4" you can use a combination of Incline Sets, Incline Starters and Risers to reach any elevation you desire.

Incline Starters are 2' long and raise the track in set increments. If you need an elevation between these increments, simply cut off the highest end of a Starter to create the correct height.

For example, a 4% Incline Starter raises the track 1" over a length of 24". If you only want to elevate the track 3/4" use only 3/4 of the 24" length or 18" of the Starter, simply cut off the last 6" from the end of the Incline Starter.

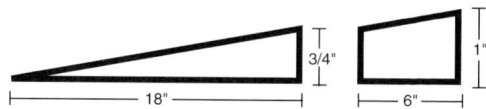

The same is true for Incline Sets. The 4% Incline Set uses 4 pieces of foam, each 24" long to raise the track 4". If you only want to raise the track 3 1/2" simply find where the Incline Set has increased to 3 1/2" and cut it off at that point.

● Create Steeper Grades

Stack 2% Incline Sets or Starters on top of 4% Incline Sets or Starters to create a 6% grade. Place 4% Starters on top of 4% Starters for an 8% grade. Remember, the steeper the grade, the more trouble the engine will have climbing. Make sure your engine will pull a train up the grade you design.

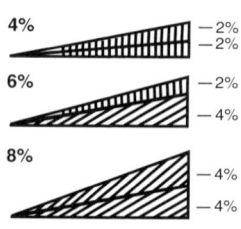

● Change Grades

Use 2% and 4% Incline Starters in combination to change grades in the middle of an Incline. Start your inclines on a 2% grade; increase to 4% in the middle of the incline; drop back down to 2% before leveling off. This will create more dramatic grades and a more realistic look.

● Rise to Any Elevation

Incline Starters and Risers are designed for elevations in even increments of 1/2" (at 2%) or 1" (at 4%). Inclines and Risers can be cut for other elevations. Suppose, for example, your track plan calls for the track to climb 1-1/4" at a 4% grade, run level for some distance, and then either rise or fall to a different elevation. Combining the appropriate Risers and Inclines is quite simple.

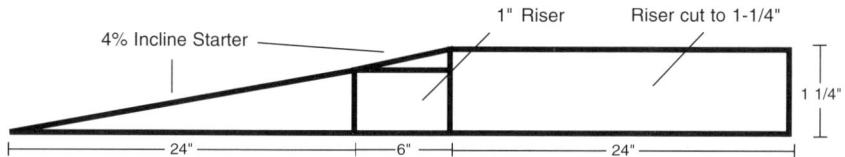

First, use a 4% Incline Starter to raise the elevation 1". Then using another 4% Incline Starter, cut off all but the first 6". This 6" portion of the Incline raises the track 1/4". Cut a 1" Riser to 6" long to place under this Starter.

Now you need Risers cut to 1-1/4" for the level, elevated area. This can be done with the Hot Wire Foam Cutter. Adjust the collars so the wire is held 1-1/4" away from the ends of the rods. Hold the Hot Wire Foam Cutter upside-down against a clean, level surface. Be sure the surface is non-metallic and will not conduct electricity. Push a 2" Riser through the Foam Cutter. This will cut the Riser to 1-1/4". You may wish to make a test cut first on a scrap piece of foam. Check the height against your Incline.

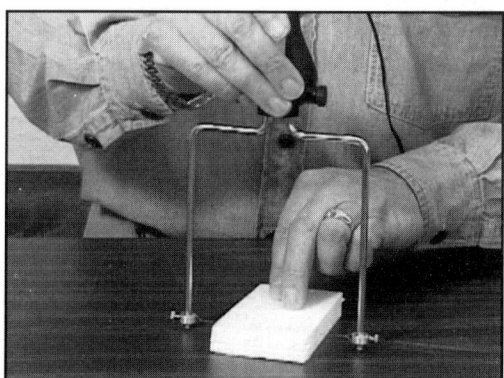

Adjust height of wire and push foam through the cutter for exact thicknesses.

46

● Banking Risers and Inclines

Real roads and railroads are often banked slightly on curves. Some modelers choose to bank their layout's roads and track to enhance realism. Insert shims under Risers or Inclines around the outside of curves. Then glue your track down normally.

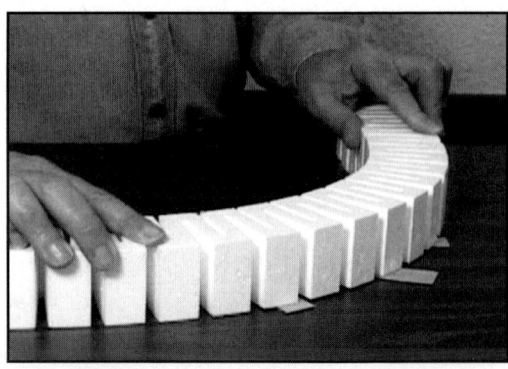

For banking the shims need to be inserted under the outside of curves before gluing in place.

● Pre-Assemble Risers and Inclines

You may also wish to simplify installation of Incline Starters and Risers by pre-assembling sections. Start with the lowest section and work toward the highest. Stack Risers and Incline Starters to desired height. Glue these together with the Low Temp Foam Glue Gun, or Foam Tack Glue. Install these preassembled sections just as you would Incline Sets.

● Model any Situation

Incline Starters and Risers can be used together to accommodate any circumstances your track plan may call for. You can stack 2% Inclines on top of 4% Inclines to form 6% Inclines. You can use 2% Inclines on a part of a 4% Incline Set to change the grade in the middle of a slope. You can stack Risers on top of Risers to form an elevated level area.

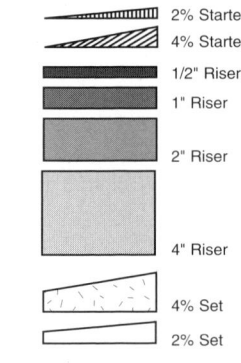

2% Starter
4% Starter
1/2" Riser
1" Riser
2" Riser
4" Riser
4% Set
2% Set

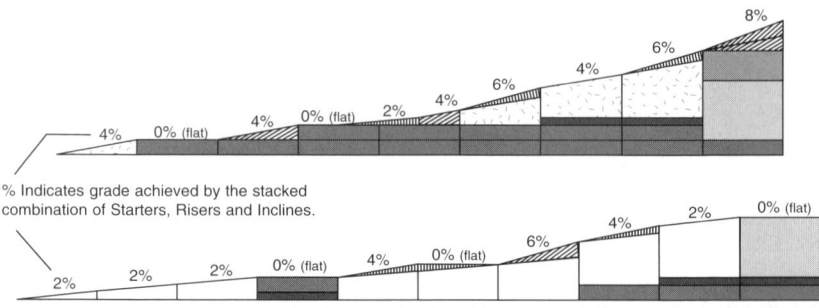

% Indicates grade achieved by the stacked combination of Starters, Risers and Inclines.

There is no limit to the situations you can create. The illustrations show many ways Risers and Inclines can be used together. It is unlikely that you will use all of these methods in a single layout. Use the Risers and Inclines in combination to make the grade you need.

B. More Ideas for the Road System

Woodland Scenics Road System is a line of products specially designed and formulated to create realistic streets, roads, sidewalks, parking lots and curbs. The Road System can be used on a new layout you are creating or to resurface roads on an existing layout.

● Building a Large Parking Area

Build a large parking area one section at a time. Lay Paving Tape around the perimeter of the parking area to be created. Break the interior into smaller sections with Paving Tape.

Fill alternate sections with Smooth-It and allow to dry. Remove Paving Tape. Use Smooth-It to fill remaining sections. Use the existing dry Smooth-It to support the Spreader Tool.

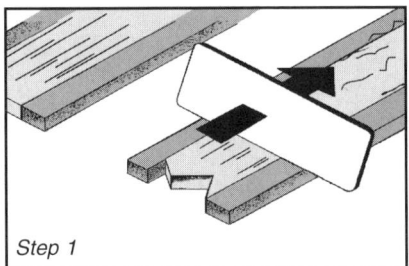
Step 1

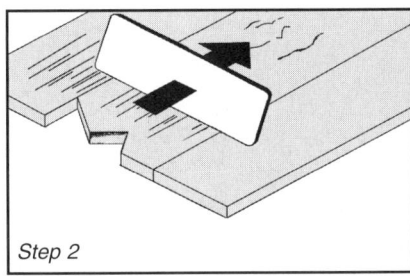
Step 2

Create a parking area by breaking the interior into small sections.

● Building Road Crossings

Road crossings are necessary wherever a street or road crosses railroad tracks.

Determine the width and position of the road, and draw it onto your hardshell as discussed in the section Using the Road System on page 40.

Where the road will cross the track the Track-Bed will need to be removed from both sides of the track. Use the Foam Knife or a hobby

48

knife to cut out and remove this material.

The finished road should be the same height as the top of the rails on your track. Cut an Incline Starter to raise the height of the road. If you are using the Woodland Scenics Road System, allow 1/16" for the thickness of the road. Once this Starter is covered with Plaster Cloth, Smooth-It

Where the road will cross the track, the Track-Bed will need to be removed from along the sides of the track.

and Top Coat it will be the right height. If you are using another system to finish your roads, the incline height might need to be slightly different.

Use one or more Incline Starters to accommodate the entire width of the road. Place Starters on each side of the road in the area where Track-Bed was removed. Push these Inclines tightly up against the track's

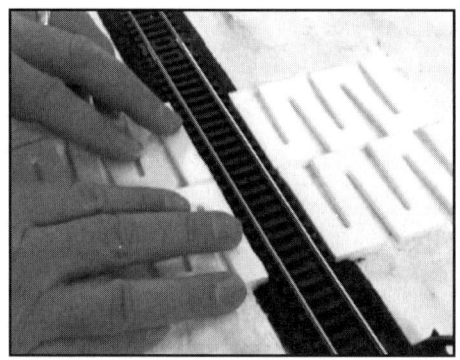

Use one or more Incline Starters to accommodate the entire road width.

ties. This will leave a small gap between the Incline and the rail. This gap will be filled later with Plaster Cloth and Smooth-It.

Lay Plaster Cloth over the Incline Starters. Blend this Plaster Cloth into the existing hardshell. Keep this Plaster Cloth off of the rails. If plaster gets on the rails it should be cleaned off with a damp rag.

Now, fill in the area between the rails. Cut two small strips of Paving Tape to fit between the rails, and place them at either side of the road crossing. Mix a small batch of Smooth-It and use it to fill in the road between the rails.

Use a Foam Knife or hobby knife to cut a thin groove in the road on the inside of the rails. This will allow the trains' wheels to pass over the road crossing. This can be done while the Smooth-It is still slightly

wet, or after it has dried.

Finish the road with Asphalt or Concrete Top Coat as described in Using the Road System on page 40.

If you prefer, you may also fill the road between the rails with a thin *styrene* strip or a piece of Foam Sheet cut and sanded to fit. Check the height of the rails for your track type, and also the width between the rails and the road's width. Be sure the styrene or foam stays back far enough from the rails to allow the train's wheels to pass without interference. This styrene or foam strip can be painted with Asphalt or Concrete Top Coat just like the rest of your roads.

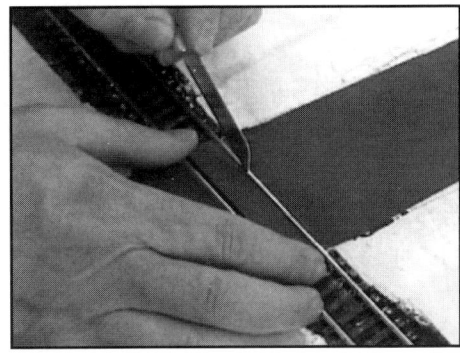

Use a hobby knife and cut a thin groove along the inside of each rail.

Finish the road with Top Coat.

C. Mixing Smooth-It and Top Coats

Concrete and Asphalt Top Coats can be mixed with Smooth-It before applying for variations in color. Each batch will be a slightly different color, so be sure to mix enough at one time to complete the whole job.

D. Using SubTerrain With Other Scales

Model railroads are generally built as scale railroads; that is: Everything on the layout is built to a specific percentage of its size in the real world. In model railroading there are a number of common scales, with engines ranging from those small enough to hold in the palm of your hand to those large enough to ride.

The selection of scale to model is entirely up to you. There are a number of items that can be considered before selecting a scale. These include the available space, how much railroad you want to work with,

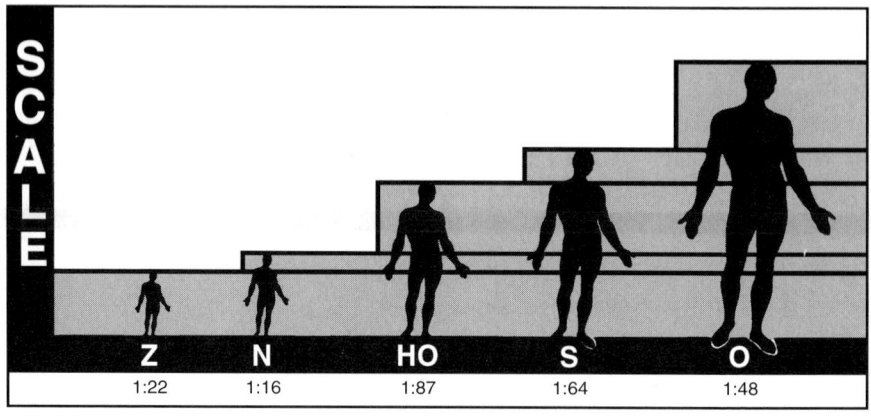

money available to put into the hobby and where the railroad is to be located. SubTerrain foam is designed to work well in most scales. Ask your dealer for more help determining which scale is right for you.

This book has focused on using SubTerrain to build an HO scale model railroad. Although HO is a very popular scale, many modelers prefer to use other common scales. SubTerrain was designed with this in mind. The SubTerrain system can be used for most scales. The most important thing to remember about using SubTerrain with other scales is that the foam components will be covered with Plaster Cloth, so modifications to the foam will not affect the appearance of your layout.

 TECH TIP

Many N scale track plans feature large sections of double track. SubTerrain Risers are slightly too narrow to accommodate this. After installing Risers and Inclines cut a 1/4" or 1/2" wide piece of Foam Sheet to glue to the sides of Risers. This will give you adequate width to support two sections of track side by side.

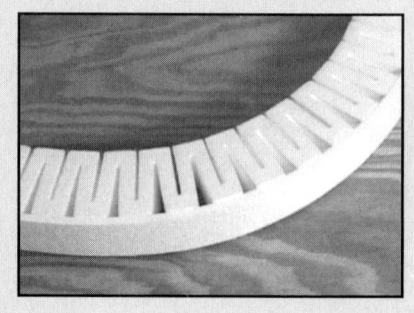

Risers or Inclines can be laid side-by-side to form a wider track base for 'larger' layouts such as O scale. Foam components can also be cut narrower or beveled for 'smaller' layouts such as N or Z scale, although this is only necessary where foam will interfere with other features of your layout such as ravines, creekbeds or the layout perimeter.

Many scenery items have no specific scale. Because trees, bushes, grass, mountains and streams all occur in a variety of sizes, Woodland Scenics scenery products can be used with most scales. Any Woodland Scenics product that is designed for a particular scale has that information listed on the product label.

● Cutting Risers/Inclines Lengthwise

Due to the unique shape of SubTerrain foam products, if you cut the Riser or Incline lengthwise prior to installation, it will fall apart. You can cut 1/4" off each side of a Riser or Incline without it falling apart. Cut two identical cardboard templates, as long as possible, up to 2' long.

Make a "sandwich" with the templates taped to the top and bottom of the Riser or Incline, and no more than 1/4" from the edge. Use the edges of the cardboard templates as guides and cut the Riser/Incline with your Hot Wire Foam Cutter.

Remember, cutting Risers and Inclines

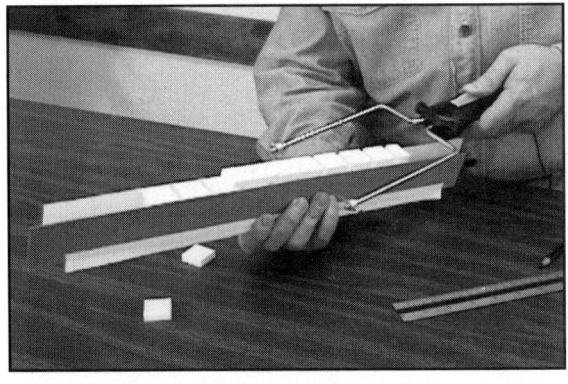

Cut two identical cardboard templates to use as a guide for cutting your Riser or Incline lengthwise.

should not be necessary unless their position interferes with other landscape features such as gullies or mountains. Normally you can simply install the SubTerrain and cover with Plaster Cloth.

● Beveling Risers and Inclines

Risers and Inclines can also be beveled at the top to provide a narrower surface for laying track. This can be especially useful for creating gullies and ditches along the track side. Bevels should be cut prior to installing foam.

Cut two identical cardboard templates, as long as possible, up to 2' long. Tape one cardboard template on top and one on the side of your Riser or Incline. These will serve as a guide for cutting your bevel, so space them back from the edge the distance to be cut out. Use the edges of the templates as guides to cut the Riser or Incline with the Hot Wire Foam Cutter.

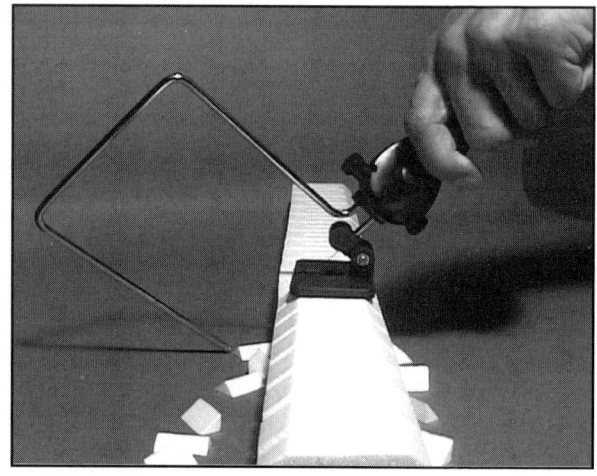

Attach the Bow and Guide to your Hot Wire Foam Cutter to cut a proper angle.

You can also use the Bow Guide to bevel foam products. Attach the *Bow and Guide* to your Hot Wire Foam Cutter. Set the angle of the guide to the angle of the bevel.

E. Split-Level Layouts

Several techniques are available for layouts that require multiple levels. Suppose your layout calls for a large town area elevated 10" above the main layout. You could easily elevate this area with Foam Sheets, bring the track to it with Inclines and use large pieces of Foam Sheets to support buildings. This is identical to the methods already presented in this book, the only difference is the total height.

It would also be possible to build a separate elevated area. Construct a 'box' out of Foam Sheets to support this area. Place this box on your layout. Use Inclines to reach this elevated area. Install Risers and

Inclines on top of this box just as you would on your plywood base. Depending on the size of this area, you may want to add additional support, use thicker Foam Sheets or create a separate plywood base.

The SubTerrain Foam System makes it easy to develop multiple levels for your layout.

F. Overpasses

A layout may call for track or roads to pass over or under each other. If your layout calls for this kind of overpass, keep in mind that you will need adequate clearance both horizontally and vertically. The amount of clearance will depend upon the scale of your layout. Check trains or vehicles that will pass through.

When creating an overpass it is important to adequately support the upper track or road. Use at least 1/2" Foam Sheets for the upper support. If gap is large you may wish to use thicker foam or hardboard for proper

When installing overpasses the amount of clearance may vary depending upon the scale of your layout.

support. Cut a piece of hardboard or Foam Sheet 2 1/2" wide (the width of a Riser) and 3" longer than the length of the opening.

Now cut notches in the tops of the Riser at either end of the overpass. These notches should be 1 1/2" long. Glue the piece of Foam Sheet into the opening you have created.

G. Creating Mountains

The easiest, cleanest way to create realistic mountains and hills in your layout is with newspaper wads and Plaster Cloth, as described in step 5 (see page 32). It is also possible to create mountains using Foam Sheets.

Cut rough contours in several pieces of Foam Sheet and stack these sheets on your layout base. Glue these sheets together with Foam Tack Glue. Some glues and solvents will melt foam products, so be sure to use a product designed to work with foam.

Allow this glue to dry thoroughly before proceeding. Use the Foam Knife, sandpaper, a file or rasp to refine your terrain contours. Sanding away this much foam will produce a lot of dust. As with burning or melting foam, this dust can be hazardous with some types of foam. SubTerrain white foam dust is nontoxic, but a dust mask or ventilator should be used to avoid inhaling dust.

Once you have created the profile you desire you can seal the foam with *Flex Paste* or Plaster Cloth. Be sure to wipe up all loose foam dust with a damp cloth before sealing or finishing your mountain. Seams and gaps between sheets of foam can be filled with *Foam Putty*.

If you want a hollow mountain you can create a mountain with newspaper wads and Plaster Cloth as described earlier. Once the Plaster Cloth has hardened the newspaper wads can be removed. Once dry, the Plaster Cloth hardshell will support itself.

Flex Paste bonds to foam, plaster, wood and other materials and forms a durable, flexible, waterproof surface when dry. Flex Paste is specially formulated for modeling; it does not shrink as it dries. Paint Flex Paste on surfaces with a clean brush.

H. Placing a Building on a Hillside

Buildings and other structures added to your layout should rest on a level surface. Often terrain has contours making it unsuitable for supporting buildings.

To place a building, cut a foam block to act as the building's foundation. This should be cut to the size and shape of the building. Draw or trace the foam block's outline onto your hardshell. Cut away the hardshell with a sharp knife. Size the hole to fit your block. Remove the hardshell and newspaper wads underneath it. Insert your foam 'foundation' and glue it in place with Low Temp Foam Glue or Foam Tack Glue.

Fine sand and coat the foundation with Flex Paste and Concrete Top Coat to give it the appearance of a concrete foundation. Mount the building on top of the foundation and glue it in place.

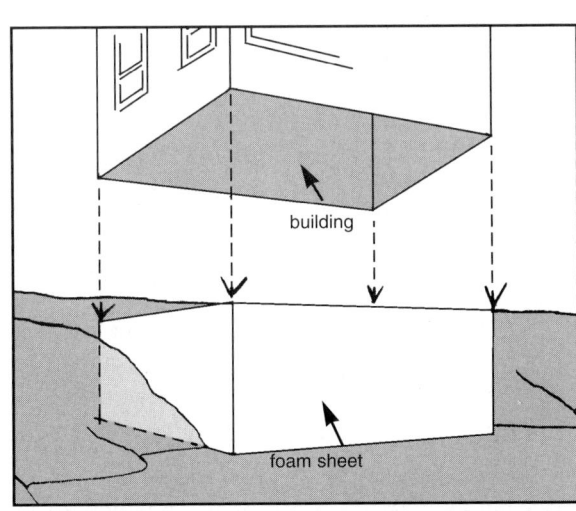

Cut into the Plaster Cloth hardshell and install foam sheet for foundation where building will be placed.

56

I. Adding to an Existing Layout

Many model railroad layouts change over time. You may wish to change your layout by adding buildings and roads. Buildings can be added as described above in Placing a Building on a Hillside. This method of cutting into the hardshell and adding a building can be used anywhere on a layout. You can also add roads in a similar manner. All of this can be done even after landscaping has been installed.

Buildings and roads can be added to an existing layout.

First determine where the road will be located. Now cut through the Plaster Cloth hardshell using a hobby knife, and remove the Plaster Cloth and any newspaper wads where the road will be located.

Use a hobby knife to remove Plaster Cloth hardshell where buildings and roads will be located.

Install Risers in place underneath the road. If necessary use newspaper wads or scrap foam to support these Risers. Glue Risers to the remaining hardshell or pin them in place with Foam Nails. Foam Nails can be left in place

Remove newspaper wads and install risers where roads will be located.

permanently, so long as they do not protrude above the new hardshell.

Cover Risers with a new layer of Plaster Cloth and blend this into the existing hardshell. If landscaping has already been installed, it might be necessary to clear some of this material away in order to properly blend the Plaster Cloth. A thin putty knife usually works well for removing landscaping material.

Cover Risers with a new layer of Plaster Cloth and blend this into the existing hardshell.

When the Plaster Cloth has dried, finish the road as described in the section Using the Road System on page 40. Replace any landscaping material that might have been removed during this process.

Replace any landscaping material that might have been removed during this process.

These techniques can be used to add buildings, roads, even additional track to any layout.

SubTerrain is great for new layouts or modifying existing layouts to form a realistic model.

58

J. Using Under the Track Switch Machines

Most *switch machines* allow a maximum of 1" of material between the switch machine and the switch or turnout. Switch machines may be installed inside the Risers. Review the manufacturer's instructions to determine the location and to ensure proper operation of the switch machine's linkage after installation.

To install an under the track switch machine simply cut a notch in the Risers and install a piece of hardboard to support the switch machine. Cut a hole in the plywood base for installation and servicing of the switch machine.

Use a piece of hardboard to support your switch machine as shown in module above.

Now you should be ready to finish the installation of the switch machine following the manufacturer's instructions.

K. Cutting Foam Circles

It is easy to cut perfect circles from Foam Sheets with the Hot Wire Foam Cutter. Use a Foam Nail to pin a piece of foam to your work table. The Foam Nail should be the same distance from the edge of the table as the radius of your circle. Hold your Hot Wire Foam Cutter against the edge of the table and rotate the piece of foam around the Foam Nail. As the foam rotates, the Hot Wire Foam Cutter will cut a perfect circle.

Rotate the Foam Sheet to form a perfect circle.

L. Elevated Buildings

Often it is important to install certain buildings, such as a depot, precisely at track height. If you have a level area prepared for this building you can use Foam Sheets under the building to bring it up to track level. 1/4" Foam Sheet is the ideal thickness for this. Cut the outline of your building in Foam Sheets of the appropriate thickness. Glue this foam directly to your hardshell. Cover this with Flex Paste. This should create a 'foundation' for your building that is elevated above your level area.

M. Cut Your Own Bridges From Foam Sheets

You can make bridges and other structures from Foam Sheets. Cut templates from piece of cardboard. Tape these templates to the sides of a piece of 3" Foam Sheet. Use your Hot Wire Foam Cutter to cut along the outlines formed by the template.

Bridges and other structures can be made from Foam Sheets.

You can also assemble a bridge from Foam Sheet pieces. Cut two sides of a bridge as described above, only use 1/2" Foam Sheets. Glue these together to form a bridge.

With either of the bridges above you can create bridge railings from 1/4" Foam

Sheets or cut thin strips with the Hot Wire Foam Cutter. You can also use styrene strips available from your hobby retailer. Paint your bridge deck with Asphalt or Concrete Top Coat. Use Concrete Top Coat to paint the sides of the bridge.

N. Mock-Up Stand-In Buildings

Often it is difficult to judge whether or not you have enough space to place a building on your layout. Nothing is more frustrating than putting together a building kit, only to discover it is too large for your layout.

Most building kits have the building's dimensions printed on the package. Simply write down these dimensions for all of the buildings on your layout before purchasing or assembling them. Use 1/4" or 1/2" Foam Sheets to cut out and assemble replicas of the buildings you wish to purchase. Arrange these on your layout. Adjust the position of any buildings that do not fit. If the buildings are not the right size, go back to your hobby store and find buildings that will fit. Now you can purchase and assemble buildings with the confidence they will fit perfectly.

Create "mock ups" to test fit your buildings.

Plan entire cities with "mock up" buildings.

If you cannot find a building that's just right for your layout, you might consider Design Preservation Model's Modular Building System. With this system you can custom design and create exactly the buildings you want for your layout.

Add More Terrain Features

SubTerrain is a complete layout construction system. It was designed to integrate with Woodland Scenics' complete line of terrain and landscaping accessories. Woodland Scenics Terrain and Landscaping Systems are the perfect way to bring your layout to life. Using these products together, anyone can create a realistic model railroad. For a complete description of the entire Woodland Scenics Terrain and Landscaping Systems refer to The Scenery Manual and The Clinic video, both available from your retailer.

Here are just a few of the simple ideas you can use to add realistic scenery to your layout.

● Install Tunnel Portals and Retaining Walls

Tunnel Portals provide a realistic facing for tunnel entrances. Retaining Walls are used to stop rock and dirt from falling on the track. Woodland Scenics Tunnel Portals and Retaining Walls are made of high-density plaster which can easily be stained or further detailed. Place Tunnel Portals at tunnel openings. Use Retaining Walls to hold back rock along steep terrain.

Stain then test fit your Plaster castings.

Stain pieces with Woodland Scenics *Earth Color Liquid Pigment* as desired and test fit in place. Plaster castings can be shaped to fit with sandpaper, a sharp knife or rasp. Attach Tunnel Portals and Retaining Walls with *Lightweight Hydrocal* or Foam Tack Glue. When using Lightweight Hydrocal, mist the plaster with water before applying for better adhesion. Gaps can be filled with Lightweight Hydrocal.

● Create Rock Outcroppings

Rock outcroppings are naturally occurring terrain features that range in size from small field rocks to large cliff faces. Rock outcroppings form

differently in different areas of the country, so be sure to consider the area your layout represents before adding rock outcroppings.

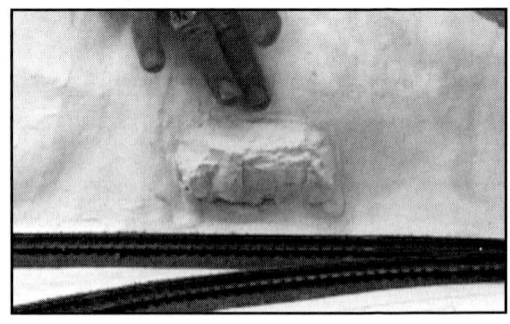

Test fit the rock outcroppings in place. Stain them with Earth Color Liquid Pigment washes. Adhere them in

Test fit rock outcroppings before adhering them in place with Lightweight Hydrocal.

place with Lightweight Hydrocal. If you prefer, you can stain or paint them after they have been affixed. Use Woodland Scenics *Talus* (rock debris) under the rock outcroppings for additional realism.

Lightweight Hydrocal is specially formulated for terrain modeling. It can be used as an extra durable coating on top of Plaster Cloth, to fill open spaces around plaster castings, cast rocks and other terrain features, and as an adhesive for joining plaster castings together. When dry, Lightweight Hydrocal can be formed with a hobby knife or sanded to an extremely smooth durable finish.

When fitting Tunnel Portals, Retaining Walls and rock outcroppings in place, it may be necessary to cut into the Plaster Cloth hardshell. If there is not a tight fit, these are easily filled with small strips of Plaster Cloth or Lightweight Hydrocal.

Create rock outcroppings with Woodland Scenics Rock Molds and Lightweight Hydrocal. You can purchase Rock Molds, or create your own using Woodland Scenics Latex Rubber. Either way, the finished rock outcroppings can be shaped and carved with sandpaper or a hobby knife.

● *Stain the Hardshell with Earth Pigment Washes*

Stain the Hardshell with Woodland Scenics Earth or Green Undercoat Liquid Pigment washes. Pigments are specifically designed for model use and include earth tones that are often difficult to find elsewhere. Use the pigments to color hardshell. Don't overdo this. A light transparent covering of pigment, with some white still showing through is sufficient. This will be covered later with Turf.

● *Ballast the Track*

All railroads use rock between the ties for stability. This rock is called Ballast. Woodland Scenics Ballast is made in several different sizes and colors. When selecting a size, be sure to consider the scale of your layout.

Pour a small quantity of Ballast down the center of the track using a Scenic

Pour a small quantity of Ballast down the center of the track.

Sifter. Use a dry, clean paintbrush to sweep the Ballast off the tops of ties and rails. Spray the Ballast with Scenic Cement to affix to Track-Bed. After Ballast has dried, remember to clean off the track with an eraser-type track cleaner to remove any traces of Ballast or Scenic Cement. If the track is not carefully cleaned, power may not get to the engines or derailments could occur when the wheels come in contact with material on the rails.

● *Plant Vegetation and Trees*

Use the complete line of Woodland Scenics products to add realistic vegetation to your layout. Start with a ground cover using Green or Earth

Refer to the Scenery Manual for a full explanation of Woodland Scenics complete line of landscaping products.

64

Blended Turf. Hold Blended Turf in place with a misting of Scenic Cement. Add variegated coloring with Fine Turf. Spray with Scenic Cement. Add more texture and realism with Coarse and Extra Coarse Turf, representing larger plants and shrubs; affix them with Scenic Cement or Hob-e-Tac. Finally, add Field Grass and Trees to complete the landscape.

● *Add Buildings, Vehicles and People*

Woodland Scenics complete Scene Kits, Trackside Scenes and Scenic Details are designed for the modeler who wants fine quality craftsmanship, intricate detail and authenticity. A full line of scenes is available from your retailer.

Woodland Scenics Scenic Detail "Gazebo" D236.

Some of the best quality building kits available at a reasonable price are those made by Design Preservation Models (DPM). They have an extensive line of highly detailed injection molded styrene building kits. You can also design and build your own buildings with DPM's modular building kits.

Woodland Scenics Terrain and Landscaping Systems are the best way to add realism and authenticity to any model railroad. The Woodland Scenics product line is so easy to use that anyone can turn a train set into a realistic model railroad.

Design Preservation Models has a variety of building kits to choose from to complete your scene.

● *Conclusion*

SubTerrain foam products were designed to allow anyone, from the beginner to the experienced modeler, to quickly and easily create a model railroad layout. This book was designed to get you started with the SubTerrain System. We know as you experiment and become familiar with SubTerrain you will find all kinds of new ways to use it. Don't keep these great ideas a secret. We want to hear about your new ideas for using SubTerrain.

Contact us: Woodland Scenics • PO Box 98 • Linn Creek, MO 65052 or subterrain@woodlandscenics.com

Appendix

The track plan used throughout this book, and in the video "SubTerrain: A How-To Video" is simple enough for anyone to build. We used this plan for demonstration purposes. Here is everything you need to know to build this layout yourself.

First you will need to purchase track. We used rigid track but this plan can be adapted to flex track. Most track comes in standard sizes and radii, but you may wish to check the specifications from your track manufacturer to be sure the pieces will fit together properly.

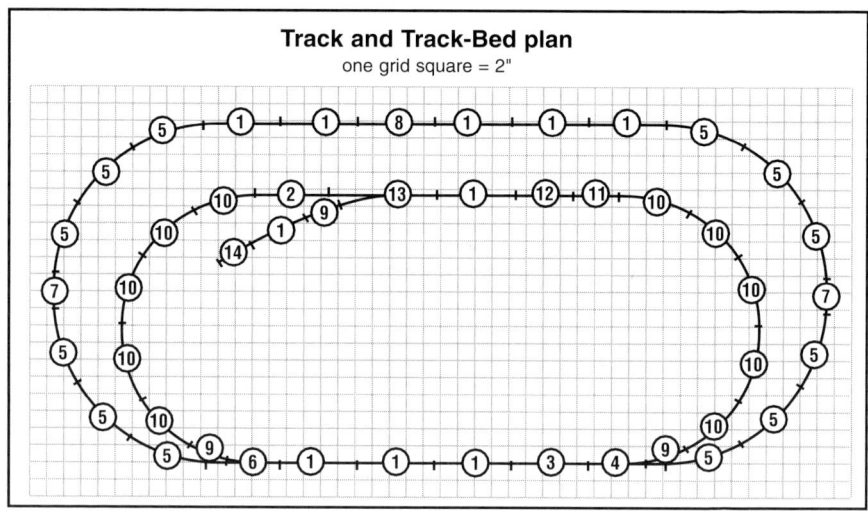

Track and Track-Bed plan
one grid square = 2"

Fixed Track Components

1 - 9" Straight ....10 pcs.	8 - 9" Terminal ....1 pc.
2 - 9" Rerailer ....1 pc.	9 - 1/2 -15" Radius ....3 pcs.
3 - Warren Truss Bridge ..1 pc.	10 - 15" Radius ....10 pcs.
4 - #4 Left Hand Turnout ..1 pc.	11 - 6" Straight ....1 pc.
5 - 18" Radius ....12 pcs.	12 - Pony Truss Bridge ......1 pc.
6 - #4 Right Hand Turnout 1 pc.	13 - #6 Left Hand Turnout ..1 pc.
7 - 3" Straight ....2 pcs.	14 - Bumper ....1 pc.

Bill of Materials

Next, you will need to purchase SubTerrain foam. Here is a list of all of the foam products you will need to complete this layout.

5 - packages of 2" Risers   **4 - packages of 1/4" Foam Sheets**
2 - packages of 4% Incline Sets **10 - packages of Plaster Cloth**
8 - packages of Profile Boards   **16 - pieces of HO Track-Bed**
8 - packages of 1" Foam Sheets

In addition you may also wish to purchase many of the SubTerrain tools, glues and accessories. A quick review of the techniques in this book should give you an idea of which tools you will need.

We used several buildings from Design Preservation Models in our layout plan. The following illustration shows the buildings we used, and where they were placed. It also shows terrain and landscape features.

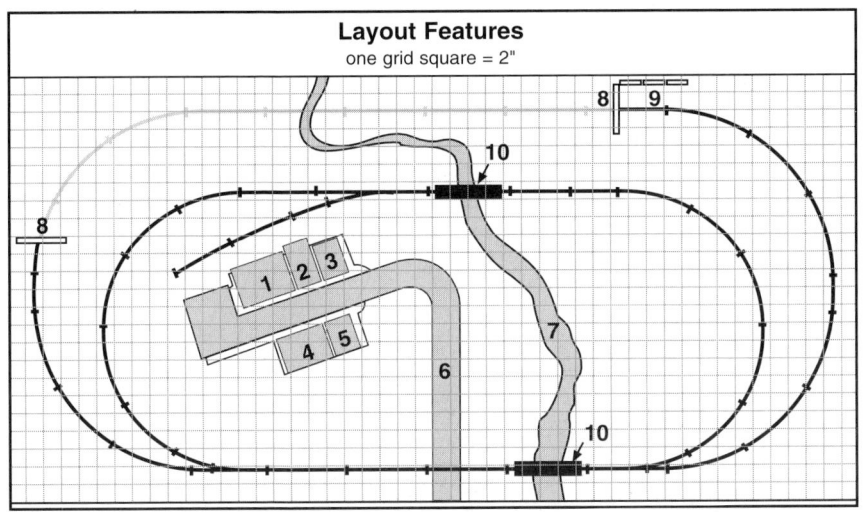

Layout Features
one grid square = 2"

Buildings

1. DPM Goodfellows Hall #108
2. DPM HO Modular Building
3. DPM Kelly's Saloon #101
4. DPM Front Street Building #120
5. DPM Kelly's Saloon #101

Terrain Features

6. Road
7. Dry Creek Bed
8. WS Tunnel Portals #C1253
9. WS Retaining Walls #C1259
10. 9" Bridges

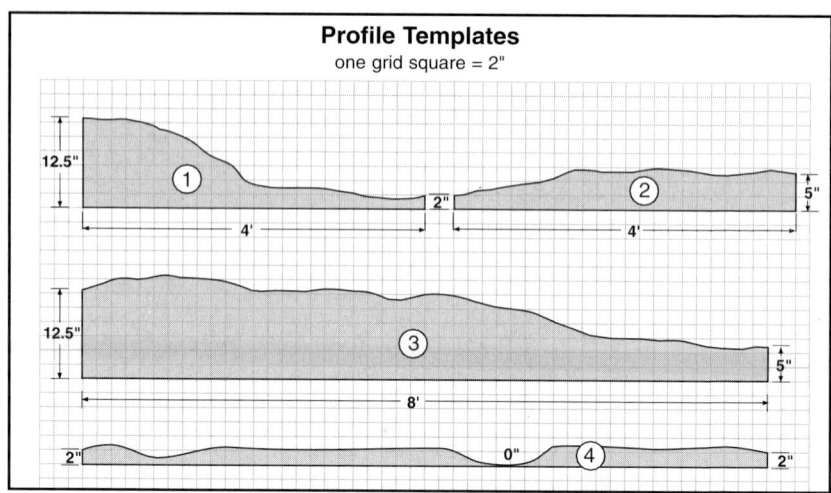

Profile Templates
one grid square = 2"

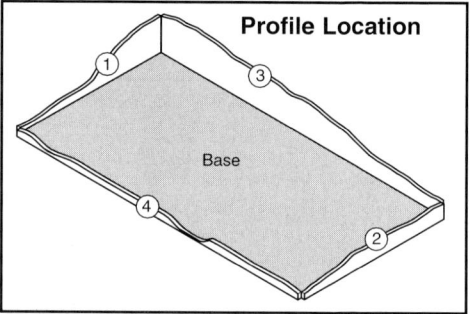

Profile Location

Base

When you are finished, you will have a realistic model railroad that will provide hours of enjoyment. Don't stop here. Now it is time to add your own touches, or start a completely new layout.

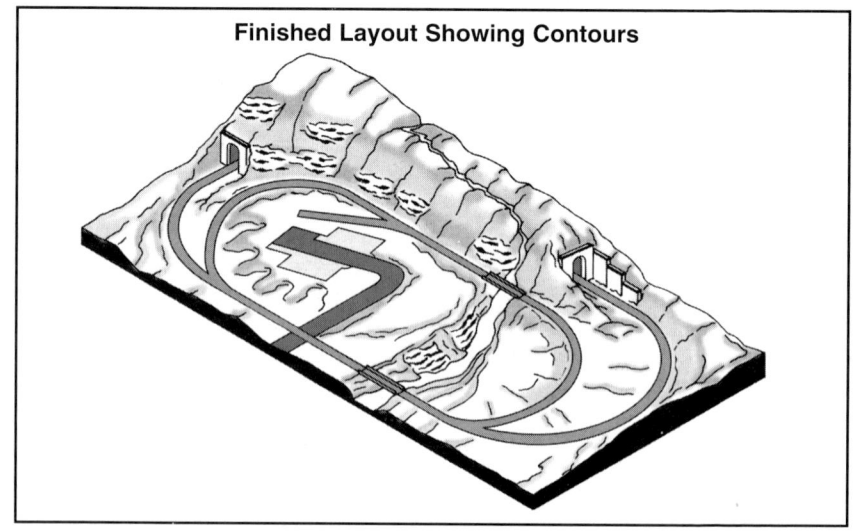

Finished Layout Showing Contours

Product Listing
Introduction

In addition to a detailed explanation of SubTerrain, this book has briefly covered a few of the products and techniques that you can use to add realism to your model railroad layout.

Woodland Scenics produces a complete line of terrain and landscaping products that anyone can use. Just like SubTerrain these products were designed with ease of use, and realistic results in mind. Anyone from the beginner to the most experienced modeler can use Woodland Scenics products.

Although the main focus of this book has been the SubTerrain product line, we know that you are not going to want to stop there.

Take a few minutes to review the overview list of Woodland Scenics landscaping and terrain products listed for you on the following pages. You will find that everything you need is available from Woodland Scenics.

Our product line is growing all the time. We are constantly researching new ways to improve our products, and to improve your layout. Look at page 71 to see how you can get a full color catalog.

The layout in this book used several buildings from Design Preservation Models. Check with your local hobby retailer. You can also get a full color catalog from DPM by sending $1.50, or 5 first class stamps to:

Design Preservation Models
PO Box 66
Linn Creek, MO   65052

They also have a complete product listing on their website at:

www.dpmkits.com

We at Woodland Scenics want to hear about your experiences with SubTerrain, and the entire line of terrain and landscaping products. Please direct your questions and comments to the address on page 66.

PRODUCT LISTING

Woodland Scenics products provide complete systems for terrain building, landscaping, and detailing your models. All of the products are easy to use and are designed to color coordinate and complement each other for the greatest possible realism. These products represent the most advanced level in the evolution of scenery-making products and techniques.

The following pages provide a partial product listing with color samples at the back. If you would like a complete catalog of all Woodland Scenics products, send five first class postage stamps or $1.50 to: Woodland Scenics, P.O. Box 98, Linn Creek, MO 65052.

The Scenery Kit (S927)

The Scenery Kit offers you the opportunity to learn the terrain and landscape building techniques needed for completing the scenery on a larger module or layout. In just a couple of evenings you will gain a wide range of skills that can be put to use improving your layout. Included are complete instructions and hardboard sides plus the Plaster Cloth, Lightweight Hydrocal, Culvert, rock castings, Earth Color Liquid Pigments, Ballast, Turf, Clump-Foliage, Poly Fiber, Talus, and Trees needed to complete this 10" X 18" display piece. Use it to show off an engine or piece of rolling stock.

71

Medium Green Foliage (F52)

Medium Green Foliage Clusters
(FC58)

Light Green Mix Lichen (L167)

TURF, COARSE TURF, EXTRA COARSE TURF, BLENDED TURF

Turf, Coarse Turf, and Extra Coarse Turf are made of ground foam material with six colors in each grade for all your landscape needs. Blended Turf comes in two fine blends for use as a base coat on landscape areas. These products give you the most realistic colors and textures allowing you to mix and blend for maximum realism.

FOLIAGE CLUSTERS*

A specially produced ground foam product ideal for creating bushes, undergrowth, and tree foliage. Available in three realistic colors.

LICHEN

A natural product which can be combined with the Turf and Foliage items to model bushes, ground cover, and foliage. Lichen is available in a variety of colors for modeling any season of the year.

SCENIC CEMENT

This ready to use matte-medium formula can be sprayed or brushed on and dries to a clear matte finish. It is a nontoxic water base cement which can be used in innumerable ways on the layout. Available in an economical 16-oz. bottle.

SCENIC SIFTER

The clear plastic Scenic Sifter comes with two interchangeable, snap-on sifter caps in different sizes making it easy to apply Ballast, Turf, Coarse Turf, and Extra Coarse Turf to the layout. Blank labels and a solid lid for storage make this the ideal way to store all the Turf and Ballast products for easy identification and availability.

SCENIC SPRAYER

Durable 8-oz. plastic bottle with a long siphon tube and spray head with nozzle that adjusts from very fine mist to a steady stream. Use for spraying water, wet water, salt water, Scenic Cement, and Earth Colors. Spray head also fits Scenic Cement bottle.

*WOODLAND SCENICS PATENTED PRODUCT

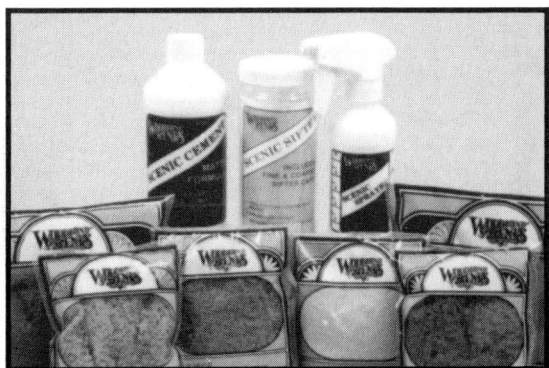
Scenic Cement (S191), Scenic Sifter (S193), Scenic Sprayer (S192)

72

FIELD GRASS

A natural hair product in four colors perfect for modeling tall grasses and weeds. Four colors are available for modeling both green and golden grasses.

POLY FIBER

This synthetic fiber can be stretched and torn to form airy, almost transparent types of ground cover. Use it for ivy, vines, and delicate plants.

TREE KITS*

The metal trunk tree kits are designed to include more detail, to take more time to build, and to have a more lacy see through look. Bend the armatures to your specifications, color them, and add the Foliage material to model particular varieties of trees or create a tree to fit a particular area.

BALLAST

Realistically model ballast on the railroad with a choice of seven colors and three sizes to fit almost any area of the country and any scale. Also use Ballast to model gravel roads, rock piles, and hopper loads.

HOB-E-TAC ADHESIVE

A multi-purpose high tack adhesive which bonds on contact. Particularly good for attaching Field Grass to the layout and making and installing trees.

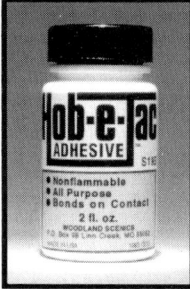

Hob-e-Tac (S195)   Field Grass (See page 146)

Five Pine Trees TK23

Poly Fiber (FP178)

Light Gray Ballast (B74)

REALISTIC TREES SELECTION GUIDE

ITEM NUMBER	ACTUAL HEIGHT	COLOR	TREES PER PKG	SCALE HEIGHT N 1/160	HO 1/87	O 1/48
GREEN DECIDUOUS						
TR1001	3/4"-1 1/4"	MED GREEN	8	10' - 17'	5' - 9'	3' - 5'
TR1002	1 1/4"-2"	MED GREEN	5	17' - 27'	9' - 15'	5' - 8'
TR1003	2" - 3"	LT GREEN	4	27' - 40'	15' - 22'	8' - 12'
TR1004	2" - 3"	MED GREEN	4	27' - 40'	15' - 22'	8' - 12'
TR1005	2" - 3"	DK GREEN	4	27' - 40'	15' - 22'	8' - 12'
TR1006	3" - 4"	LT GREEN	3	40' - 53'	22' - 29'	12' - 16'
TR1007	3" - 4"	MED GREEN	3	40' - 53'	22' - 29'	12' - 16'
TR1008	3" - 4"	DK GREEN	3	40' - 53'	22' - 29'	12' - 16'
TR1009	4" - 5"	LT GREEN	3	53' - 67'	29' - 36'	16' - 20'
TR1010	4" - 5"	MED GREEN	3	53' - 67'	29' - 36'	16' - 20'
TR1011	4" - 5"	DK GREEN	3	53' - 67'	29' - 36'	16' - 20'
TR1012	5" - 6"	LT GREEN	2		36' - 44'	20' - 24'
TR1013	5" - 6"	MED GREEN	2		36' - 44'	20' - 24'
TR1014	5" - 6"	DK GREEN	2		36' - 44'	20' - 24'
TR1015	6" - 7"	LT GREEN	2		44' - 51'	24' - 28'
TR1016	6" - 7"	MED GREEN	2		44' - 51'	24' - 28'
TR1017	6" - 7"	DK GREEN	2		44' - 51'	24' - 28'
TR1018	7" - 8"	MED GREEN	2		51' - 58'	28' - 32'
TR1019	8" - 9"	MED GREEN	2		58' - 65'	32' - 36'
FALL DECIDUOUS						
TR1040	1 1/4"-3"	FALL MIX	9		9' - 22'	5' - 12'
TR1041	3" - 5"	FALL MIX	6		22' - 36'	12' - 20'
CONIFERS						
TR1060	2 1/2"-4"	CON GREEN	5		18' - 29'	10' - 16'
TR1061	4" - 6"	CON GREEN	4		29' - 44'	16' - 24'
TR1062	6" - 7"	CON GREEN	3		44' - 51'	24' - 28'
TR1063	7" - 8"	CON GREEN	3		51' - 58'	28' - 32'

REALISTIC TREE KIT SELECTION GUIDE

ITEM	ACTUAL HEIGHT	COLOR	TREES PER PKG	SCALE HEIGHT N 1/160	HO 1/87	O 1/48
TREES						
TR1101	3/4" - 3"	LT, MED,	36	10' - 40'	5' - 22'	3' - 12'
TR1102	3" - 5"	DARK	14	40' - 67'	22' - 36'	12' - 20'
TR1103	5" - 7"	GREEN	7	67' - 93'	36' - 51'	20' - 28'
PINES						
TR1104	2 1/2" - 4"	CONIFER	42	33' - 53'	18' - 29'	10' - 16'
TR1105	4" - 6"	GREEN	24	53' - 80'	29' - 44'	16' - 24'
TR1106	6" - 8"		16	80' - 106'	44' - 58'	24' - 32'

READY MADE REALISTIC TREES*

The quickest and easiest way to add well-detailed realistic trees to your layout is with Woodland Scenics Ready Made Realistic Trees. There are 25 different packages of trees to give you all the variety you need in three shades of green deciduous trees, dark green conifer trees, and fall color deciduous trees. Each package contains between two and nine trees depending on size. Each tree is hand crafted so each is unique. If you want to model a particular variety of tree and want a little less foliage, just pluck a little off.

REALISTIC TREE KITS*

The Realistic Tree Kits give you the same type of tree as Ready Made Realistic Trees, only in kit form. It's the way to quickly, easily, and economically fill your layout with trees. Realistic Tree Kits come in six different varieties of both deciduous and conifer trees in a selection of sizes. You will be able to create up to 42 trees per kit depending on size. The plastic trunk comes packaged flat so you can bend and shape it to whatever form you want. If you wish you can even add extra detailing to simulate a particular type of tree. Then attach the Clump-Foliage to create exactly the shape of tree you want with the amount of foliage you prefer.

CLUMP-FOLIAGE (PATENT PENDING)

A ground foam product produced in the ideal size to create bushes, ground cover, and foliage for trees. Available in six realistic colors including a fall mix.

Realistic Tree Kit, 36 Trees ¾"-3"(TR1101)

TUNNEL LINER FORM

Each pour of Lightweight Hydrocal in this mold creates half of a single or double track tunnel with realistic rock walls and ceilings.

EARTH COLOR KIT

The economical way to use the Earth Color system for coloring plaster castings. Kit includes eight colors of pigment, mixing tray, foam applicator, and instructions.

E-Z WATER

This heat-activated water modeling product is clear, nearly colorless, nontoxic, low odor.

LIGHTWEIGHT HYDROCAL

A specially formulated plaster product for use in making plaster castings and hard shell. Half the weight of Hydrocal, yet dries to a tough surface which can be easily carved.

MOLD-A-SCENE PLASTER

Mix with water to form a workable plaster that is shaped like modeling clay. Dries to a hard plaster surface.

PLASTER CLOTH

The quick easy way to create a terrain shell on top of newspaper wad contours. Cut to desired size, dip in water, and place on the contours. Dries to a hard plaster surface.

LATEX RUBBER

Ready to use latex rubber for modelers who want to make their own rock molds.

FLEX PASTE

A specially formulated flexible modeling paste which will not crack as it dries. Excellent for finishing Styrofoam.

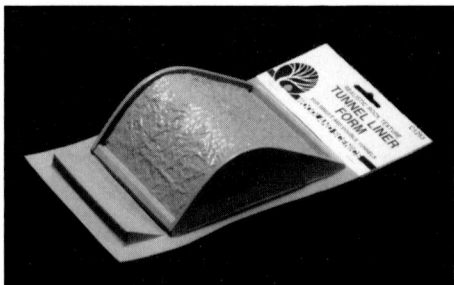
Tunnel Liner Form (C1250)

Earth Color Kit (C1215)

E-Z Water (C1206)

Lightweight Hydrocal (C1201), Mold-A-Scene Plaster (C1202), Plaster Cloth (C1203)

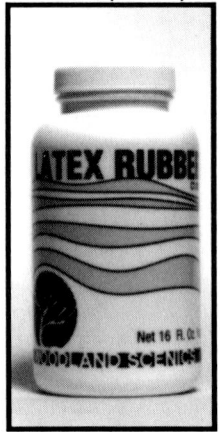
Latex Rubber (C1204)

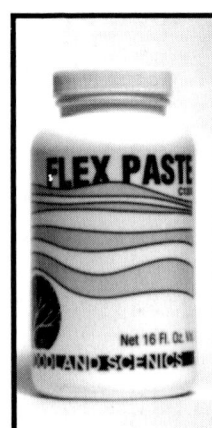
Flex Paste (C1205)

ne Talus   Medium Talus   Coarse Talus   Extra Coarse Talus

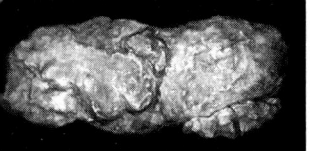

'ashed Rock (C1242)

TALUS (ROCK DEBRIS)

Talus is the rock debris that is seen almost everywhere near rocky areas, in and near water, and on top of tunnel portals and retaining walls. Model this feature with four colors and four sizes of lightweight Talus (Rock Debris) suitable for any scale. Mix the various sizes of Talus for the most realism. Select a color which most closely matches your rock areas or custom color your own Talus using the Natural color with the Earth Color Liquid Pigments.

ROCK MOLDS

The fifteen selections of Woodland Scenics Rock Molds give you the variety you need to create rocks for any area of the country, any type of terrain, and any scale. Use Lightweight Hydrocal to pour the rocks and create castings which can be carved easily with a hobby knife or dental pick. The Rock Molds are durable enough for any number of castings yet flexible enough to give you easy release of the Lightweight Hydrocal castings. The rocks you create with these molds are highly detailed for use by even the most demanding modeler.

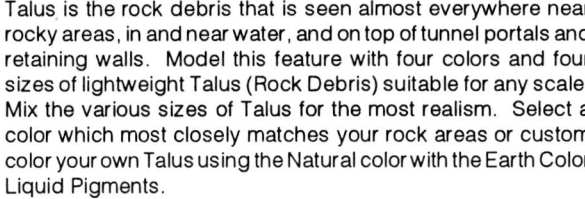

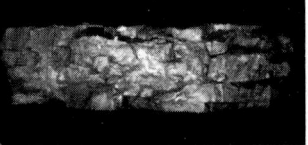

ase Rock (C1243)

acet Rock (C1244)

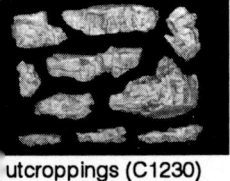 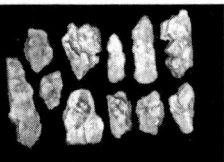 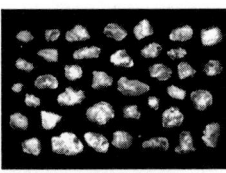 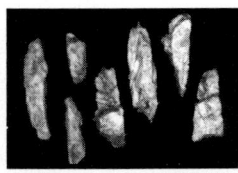

utcroppings (C1230)   Surface Rock (C1231)   Boulders (C1232)   Embankments (C1233)

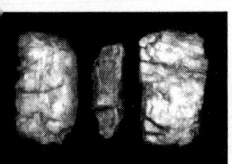 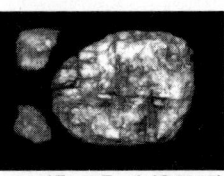  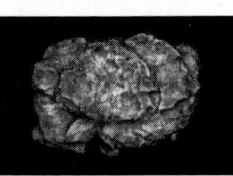

andom Rock (C1234)   Laced Face Rock (C1235)   Classic Rock (C1236)   Wind Rock (C1237)

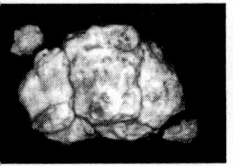 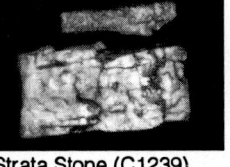 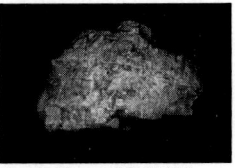 

'eathered Rock (C1238)   Strata Stone (C1239)   Rock Mass (C1240)   Layered Rock (C1241)

76

RETAINING WALLS

High density plaster Retaining Walls come three to a package. Use as is or modify to create stepped walls and curved walls. Use alone or butted together for a longer wall. Four styles add variety and detail. The Retaining Walls match the Tunnel Portal styles.

CULVERTS

Easy to assemble Culverts can be used to detail terrain areas under railroad tracks and roads. Each package contains two Culverts for use on either side of the track or road.

TUNNEL PORTALS

Tunnel Portals are useful for finishing out tunnels wherever they occur on the layout. Available varieties fit any geographic area or time era. Select from single or double track width. Use alone or with the matching Retaining Walls.

Concrete (C1258)

Cut Stone (C1259)

Concrete (C1262)

Timber (C1265)

Random Stone (C1255)

Timber Single (C1254)

Timber (C1260)

Concrete Double (C1256)

Cut Stone Single (C1253)

Random Stone (C1261)

77

Cut Stone Double Tunnel Portal (C1257)

Random Stone Culvert (C1264)

Masonry Arch Culvert (C1263)

Concrete Single Tunnel Portal (C1252) with Concrete Retaining Walls (C1258)

SCENIC DETAILS®

The Scenic Details kits give you over 40 well-designed ways to add realistic detail to your HO layout. Each of the Scenic Details contains white metal castings which are highly detailed and ready to assemble and paint. Complete instructions are included as well as any Dry Transfers or other accessories which are needed. These kits are the easy and inexpensive way to add one building or vehicle, or a whole scene to your layout. The combinations are limited only by your imagination.

Street and Traffic Lights (D248)

Tank Truck (Diamond T) (D242)

Rocky's Tavern (D238), Ice House (D219), Grain Truck (1914 Diamond T) (D218)

Hyster Logging Cruiser and Tractor (D246)

These small town scenes are created from some of the items available in the Scenic Details line. In the photo above are the Branch Line Water Tower (D241), Grain Truck (D218), and Flag Depot (D239). Below: Scenic Details can be used in almost unlimited combinations to create both town and rural scenes. The Flat Bed & Tractor (D244), left, are parked in front of the Pharmacy (D221). Next door is the Ticket Office (D222). The Sign Painter (M105), from the Mini-Scenes, completes his work. On the right is the Gas Station (D223) and Vending Machine (D230) with the Tank Truck (D242) making a delivery.

Tommy's Treehouse (M107)

Floyd's Barber Shop (M111)

Outhouse Mischief (M108)

Otis Coal Co. (TS153)

MINI-SCENES

The twelve individual Mini-Scenes include one building or other small scene to use on the railroad or as a separate display piece. All the intricate detail of the larger scenes is present, only they take up less room on the layout. Includes white metal castings plus detail items, Trees, Turf, and Foliage. Pictured above are three examples from 12 available Mini-Scenes.

COMPLETE SCENE KITS & TRACKSIDE SCENES

Designed for the modeler looking for fine quality craftsmanship, intricate detail, and authenticity. Each is a complete scene and includes the white metal castings, Turf, Foliage, and detail items needed to finish the scene. Otis Coal Co., pictured above, is one of several kits available.

DRY TRANSFER DECALS

Hundreds of signs, company logos, advertising posters, letters, numbers, and car marking data for accurately detailing any facet of the railroad. Easy to use, even for beginners. Just place in desired position and rub gently with a burnisher or dull pencil. Will adhere to a smooth or textured surface leaving no unsightly film.

MODEL GRAPHICS

Includes a 64-sheet selection of dry transfer decals which contain 340 different alphabets, number sets, and line assortments to satisfy the expert craftsman.

These photos show some differences created in landscape areas with various landscape products. Both photos show the same terrain area with rocks from the Rock Molds, the Timber Single Tunnel Portal (C1254), and Timber Retaining Walls (C1260). In the top photo, Clump-Foliage and Foliage Clusters are used to model the vegetation. The bottom photo has Ready Made Realistic Conifer Trees in various sizes.

TURF

Soil
T41

Burnt Grass
T44

Earth
T42

Green Grass
T45

Yellow Grass
T43

Weeds
T46

COARSE TURF

Earth
T60

Light Green
T63

Yellow Grass
T61

Medium Green
T64

Burnt Grass
T62

Dark Green
T65

EXTRA COARSE TURF

Yellow Grass
T34

Medium Green
T37

Burnt Grass
T35

Dark Green
T38

Light Green
T36

Conifer Green
T39

BLENDED TURF

Green Blend
T49

Earth Blend
T50

BALLAST

Iron Ore
B70

Lt. Gray
B74

Dark Brown
B71

Gray
B75

Brown
B72

Cinders
B76

Buff
B73

Coal
B92

GRAY BLEND BALLAST

Medium
B94

TALUS (ROCK DEBRIS)

EACH COLOR IS AVAILABLE IN FOUR
GRADES: FINE, MEDIUM, COARSE AND
EXTRA COARSE.

Natural
C1284

Gray
C1280

Buff
C1272

Brown
C1276

LICHEN

1½ QUART SIZE PACKAGE

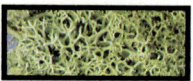

Spring Green
L161

Dark Green
L164

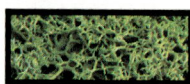

Light Green
L162

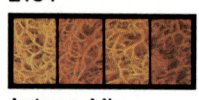

Autumn Mix
L165

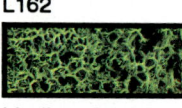

Medium Green
L163

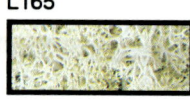

Natural
L166

3 QUART SIZE PACKAGE

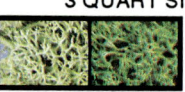

Light Green Mix
L167

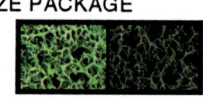

Dark Green Mix
L168

EARTH COLOR LIQUID PIGMENT

White
C1216

Black
C1220

Concrete
C1217

Raw Umber
C1221

Stone Gray
C1218

Burnt Umber
C1222

Slate Gray
C1219

Yellow Ocher
C1223

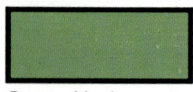

Green Undercoat
C1228

Earth Undercoat
C1229

FOLIAGE

Light Green
F51

Medium Green
F52

Dark Green
F53

Conifer Green
F54

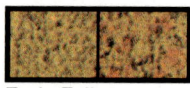

Early Fall
F55

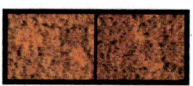

Late Fall
F56

FIELD GRASS

Natural Straw
FG171

Harvest Gold
FG172

Light Green
FG173

Medium Green
FG174

REALISTIC TREES

Light Green

Medium Green

Dark Green

Conifer Green

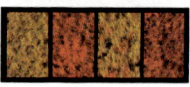

Fall Mix

FOLIAGE CLUSTERS

Light Green
FC57

Medium Green
FC58

Dark Green
FC59

POLYFIBER

Green
FP178

85

Glossary

Access hole - Access holes are used to reach covered areas of your layout. Any place a tunnel or other obstruction makes it difficult to reach your track, cut an access hole in your layout's perimeter. If your train derails in the tunnel you can easily reach through the access hole to correct the problem.

Asphalt Top Coat (ST1453) - See Top Coat.

Ballast (B70 - B94) - Real railroads use rock called ballast between the railroad ties to add stability to the ties and rails. Usually this material was taken from a nearby source. Often as tunnels were excavated or as the landscape was sculpted to make way for the track, the rock debris was saved and used for ballast. In other cases rock was quarried nearby.

Woodland Scenics Ballast comes in a wide variety of sizes and colors to reproduce ballast used in various areas of the country, and various scales. Choose the Ballast that works best for your layout.

Beveled - Cut at an angle other than 90°. Track-Bed is beveled at the edges, making it wider at the bottom than at the top. Risers and Inclines can be beveled along one or both sides to make them wider at the bottom than at the top.

Bow and Guide (ST1437) - The Hot Wire Foam Cutter can be used with the optional Bow attachment. This works well when cutting Profile Boards. The Guide allows you to make accurate cuts at any angle. The guide can also be used with the rods which come with the Hot Wire Foam Cutter.

Cable ties - Small plastic strip, used to neatly bundle wires together. These are often also referred to as zip ties. Cables ties are usually available at electronics supply stores.

Concrete Top Coat (ST1454) - See Top Coat.

Connectors - Connectors rigidly lock two or more Profile Boards together. Connectors are packaged with Profile Boards.

Contact Cement - A special type of glue that bonds on contact. Contact cement is applied to two surfaces that should be joined together. The contact cement then is allowed to dry to the touch before the two pieces of material are brought together. When the two pieces are brought together the cement bonds instantly. No additional pinning or clamping is required.

Dry Brush - A technique of adding very little paint by brushing most of the paint off a brush before using it.

Earth Color Liquid Pigments (C1215 - C1229) - Woodland Scenics sells a wide color range of pigments that are difficult to find elsewhere. These colors are specifically designed for landscape modeling.

Elevation - Elevation is the vertical distance between two points. When constructing a model railroad often the track climbs and descends hills as it moves through the landscape. The landscape itself rolls and undulates. As the track rises or falls through terrain it changes elevation.

Flex Paste (C1205) - Flex Paste is a specially formulated modeling paste. When dry Flex Paste is flexible, and therefore will not crack. It is also non-porous, and is ideal for sealing Plaster Cloth, Lightweight Hydrocal and other porous materials. Flex Paste is perfect for use as a filler, surfacer, sealer or primer.

Foam Knife (ST1433) - The Woodland Scenics Foam Knife was designed with a special 2" blade which makes it perfect for cutting foam. Most other hobby knives have a short blade, making them useless for making deep, accurate cuts in thick pieces of foam.

Foam Nails (ST1432) - Foam Nails are 2" long steel pins used to temporarily hold wood, foam, cork, cloth, plastic, track and other products together. Foam Nails are ideal for many crafts. Whenever you need to temporarily pin something together use a Foam Nail.

Because Foam Nails are nickel plated steel they can also be used as a permanent fastener. Use them for dried flower arranging, butterfly collecting or sewing and quilting. Foam Nails have unlimited uses.

Foam Pencils (ST1431) - Foam Pencils allow you to draw on foam without causing any damage. The colors will not bleed through paint or other coverings. Each package contains 2 red and 2 black pencils.

Foam Putty (ST1447) - Foam Putty is a lightweight filling compound designed to complement SubTerrain foam. It has the same characteristics as foam and can be sanded just like foam. Use Foam Putty to fill and smooth gaps and rough spots in foam. When dry, Foam Putty has the same characteristics as SubTerrain white foam. It can be sanded with fine (220 - 320 grit) sandpaper or sculpted.

Foam Sheets (ST1422 - ST1427) - Woodland Scenics white foam is available in 1' x 2' sheets in 1/4", 1/2", 1", 2", 3" and 4" thicknesses. These sheets can be used for a variety of purposes. Many craft projects use foam.

Woodland Scenics Foam Sheets are a special composite of high density, highly fused expanded polystyrene. Like all white SubTerrain foam, Woodland Scenics Foam Sheets are perfectly safe to cut with a Hot Wire Cutter. Other types of foam emit varying levels of toxic fumes and ozone depleting chemicals when cut with a hot wire cutter, melted or burned. Woodland Scenics white foam is nontoxic. Because SubTerrain foam is safe to cut, it is the first choice of many modelers.

Foam Tack Glue (ST1444) - Foam Tack Glue is specially formulated glue is high tack and effective on most materials. Use as a contact cement whenever bonding two large surfaces.

Grade - Changes in elevation on a track or road are measured by the steepness of the incline. This is referred to as the grade of an incline. The larger the grade, the steeper the incline.

Grade is simple to calculate. Take the total rise (change in elevation) of the incline in inches and divide by the total run of the incline in inches. This ratio is your grade. Grade is usually expressed as a percentage. For example, if your track rises 3 inches over a total track length of 75 inches, calculate the grade as $3 \div 75 = .04 = 4\%$. This would be a 4% grade.

Guide - See Bow & Guide.

Hardshell - Hardshell is the Plaster Cloth covering used for supporting Track-Bed, track, landscaping and terrain features. Hardshell represents the earths crust on your layout.

Hot Wire Foam Cutter (ST1435) - Woodland Scenics Hot Wire Foam Cutter is specially designed to cut SubTerrain white foam. The Hot Wire Foam Cutter comes with rods and collars, and can be used in a variety of ways to make clean, accurate cuts in foam. For additional versatility get the optional Bow and Guide attachments.

Because some foam products emit varying levels of toxic fumes when heated, melted or burned, we recommend using the Hot Wire Foam Cutter only on SubTerrain white foam. All SubTerrain white foam products are made from a special formulation of expanded polystyrene, and emit no toxic fumes when cut with a hot wire.

Incline - An incline is a change in elevation on your track or road, a hill.

Incline Set (ST1410 - ST1411) - SubTerrain's patented Incline Sets are precut foam pieces used to raise your track elevation 4". Incline Sets include all of the foam pieces necessary to raise your track in 2 or 4% grades.

Incline Starter (ST1412 - ST1413) - SubTerrain's patented Incline Starters are precut foam pieces used to raise your track either 1/2" (at 2%) or 1" (at 4%).

Landscape - The plants and trees that cover an area.

Lightweight Hydrocal (C1201) - Woodland Scenics Lightweight Hydrocal is a lightweight plaster material that was specially formulated for modelers and craftsmen. It dries to a smooth finish that is perfect for making detailed rock castings.

Low Temp Foam Glue (ST1446) - Specially formulated Low Temp Foam Glue sticks are designed to work with Woodland Scenics Low Temp Foam Glue Gun. Low Temp Foam Glue will bond to most materials. This glue will not melt SubTerrain foam, when used in the Low Temp Foam Glue Gun.

Low Temp Foam Glue Gun (ST1445) - The Low Temp Foam Glue Gun and Low Temp Foam Glue are designed to work directly on Subterrain foam and other foam products. Because the gun operates at a lower temperature than standard glue guns, it will not melt foam or plastic.

Mitered - Cut at an angle. Profile Board can be mitered at the corners where they come together. By cutting each end off at 45°, the two boards will fit snugly together with no gaps.

Modular Layout - Often several modelers join together to build a model railroad. Each modeler completes a portion of the layout. These individual section are designed to fit together with other modules to form a larger layout. This arrangement often allows modelers with limited space or resources to construct a much larger layout than would be possible individually.

NMRA (National Model Railroad Association) - An organization of people interested in model railroading as a hobby, and of manufacturers and retailers of model railroading equipment. For membership information, contact NMRA, Inc., 4121 Cromwell Rd., Chattanooga, TN 37421.

Nichrome Wire (ST1436) - Woodland Scenics Hot Wire Foam Cutter uses a special wire to cut foam. You should only use Woodland Scenics Replacement Wire with your Hot Wire Foam Cutter. Replacement wire is sold in 4' lengths.

Paving Tape (ST1455) - Paving Tape is 1/16" foam tape, with adhesive on one side. Use Paving Tape to outline streets and roads, then fill with Smooth-It. Paving tape comes with a spreader.

Plaster Cloth (C1203) - Plaster impregnated cloth used to cover terrain. Once wet, Plaster Cloth dries to a hard porous surface which provides a strong base for your track and landscaping, without the need for additional plaster.

Porous - Able to absorb water or other liquids.

Profile Boards (ST1419) - Molded foam sheets designed to interlock and stack. Profile Boards are used to surround your layout's perimeter and support terrain contours. Profile Boards and Connectors are sold together. Each package contains 2 Profile Boards and 2 Connectors.

Rail joiners - Connector used to join two pieces of sectional or flexible track together. Rail joiners provide a mechanical connection, and also provide an electrical connection for current flow. Insulated rail joiners provide a solid mechanical connection, while blocking the flow of current from one section of the track to another.

For more information on using rail joiners and wiring your track refer to your track manufacturers instructions, or one of the many books available on wiring your track.

Relief - Changes in elevation of a landscape.

Retaining Wall (C1158 - C1161 & C1258 - C1261) - Stone, brick, wood or concrete wall used to hold back dirt and rock along a steep hillside or cliff face. Woodland Scenics Retaining Walls come in a variety of styles on both N and HO scale.

Riser (ST1406 - ST1409) - SubTerrain Risers are used to elevate track and provide for more interesting terrain relief. Risers are also used in conjunction with Incline Starters to raise track to any elevation.

Roadbed - In a real railroad the roadbed is the material underneath the track used to support the track. In modeling the term roadbed is often used to refer to the material placed directly beneath the track. See Track-Bed.

Rock Outcropping - A sheer rock face protruding from a hillside or cliff. Rock outcroppings occur differently in different parts of the country. Woodland Scenics sells a variety of Rock Molds (C1230 - C1244) to create your own rock formations. You can also create your own Rock Molds with Latex Rubber (C1204).

Scale - A proportion between two sets of dimensions, i.e., the proportion between the size of a model and the dimensions of a real train, building, person, or landscape feature.

Shims - Thin often tapered pieces of material used to fill in space between things for support or leveling.

Smooth-It (ST1452) - Smooth-It is a plaster material used to create streets, roads, sidewalks, curbs, foundations, parking lots and to smooth rough spots in your hardshell.

Styrene - Styrene is a plastic often used in modeling. Many buildings and other structures are molded from styrene plastic. Styrene is also available from many hobby retailers in various sheet sizes and can be used to construct custom made model components.

Switch - Special track section used to turn an engine or car from one track to another.

Switch machine - Electrical or electronic device used to throw a switch.

Talus (C1270 - C1285) - Rock debris. Usually talus is found at the bottom of cliffs and rock outcroppings. Woodland Scenics Talus is available in a variety of sizes and colors to fit your needs.

Terrain - The physical features (such as hills and valleys) of a tract of land.

Throwbars - Most switches have a bar or bars that connect the rails and move them from one track to the other. These bars are called throwbars.

Top Coat (ST1453 & ST1454) - Woodland Scenics Asphalt and Concrete Top Coats are specially formulated coloring and protective compounds. They are used to coat the surface of any material to create realistic appearing roads, streets, sidewalks, curbs, building foundations, parking lots and retaining walls. Any relatively smooth surface can be coated with Asphalt or Concrete Top Coat to give it the appearance of real asphalt or concrete.

Track plan - A detailed diagram of a layout. The track plan usually includes the track itself, as well as details about the terrain, scenery and other features that make up the layout. Track plans are available from a variety of sources and have varying levels of detail.

Track-Bed (ST1461, ST1462, ST1471 & ST1472) - Woodland Scenics Track-Bed is placed between your hardshell and your track. Track-Bed helps smooth out imperfections in your layout base. Track-Bed is resilient, and absorbs sound and vibrations, making it the perfect product for supporting your track. Track-Bed is sold in a variety of scales. It can be purchased in packages or individual pieces.

Tunnel Portal (C1252 - C1257) - Rock, brick, wood or concrete support structure built around the opening or entrance to a tunnel. Woodland Scenics Tunnel Portals, available in many sizes and styles, are lightweight cast plaster which realistically dress the entrance to any tunnel.

Turnout - See switch.

Zip ties - See Cable ties

Index

G

H

I

L

S

V

W

Z